Information for the reader

KW-299-404

This edition of European Community environment legislation was compiled on the basis of the official texts in force most of which were published in the Official Journal of the European Communities between 1 October 1991 and 30 June 1994. A number of previous texts, omitted in the preceding edition, have been included in the present edition and are published in German, English, Danish, Spanish, French, Greek, Italian, Dutch and Portuguese.

The laws are presented in chronological order of adoption. If applicable, the principal legislation is directly followed by the amending legislation. Occasionally, technical Annexes have been deleted for reasons of their length and the highly technical information provided for specialists who have access to these texts in other publications. These deletions are indicated at the end of each act concerned.

The EEC Treaty establishes different requirements for each type of Community legislation to become effective:

- Regulations take effect on the date specified in them or, failing this, on the twentieth day following their publication in the Official Journal of the European Communities;

- Directives and decisions must be notified to those they are addressed to and take effect upon their notification. Directives often give a deadline by which the Member State must have implemented them;

- International treaties take effect when they have been ratified by a certain number of States.

Every effort has been taken to assure the completeness and accuracy of the legislation presented herein. Neither the editor nor the institutions of the EC will assume any liability for its usage.

90 0346646 1

European Community environment legislation

Volume 7 — Water

WITHDRAWN
FROM
UNIVERSITY OF PLYMOUTH
LIBRARY SERVICES

Univ

Subje

ht

mission

ate-General XI

nvironment, Nuclear Safety and Civil Protection

Cataloguing data can be found at the end of this publication

UNIVERSITY OF PLYMOUTH
Item No.   900   3466461
Date   17 MAR 1998   S
Class No. 344·046 343094 EUR
Contl. No. 9282768910
LIBRARY SERVICES

Luxembourg: Office for Official Publications of the European Communities, 1996

ISBN 92-827-6891-0 (Volume 7)
ISBN 92-827-6828-7 (Volumes 1-7)

© ECSC-EC-EAEC, Brussels · Luxembourg, 1996

Reproduction is authorized, except for commercial purposes, provided the source is acknowledged

Printed in Belgium

Table of contents

Table of contents

Preface

Legislation has long been the main pillar of the European Union's environment policy. As long ago as 1973, when environmental action first got under way, the Commission adopted a large number of measures aimed at protecting the environment and combating pollution. More often than not these were directives setting limits for emissions and standards for environmental quality, and requiring governments to help implement plans, projects and programmes for safeguarding the environment and for regulating industrial activities and products.

Environmental legislation gathered pace during the 1980s: the completion of the Single Market meant that environmental rules and standards had to be harmonised to allow goods and services to move freely between the Member States.

At the same time, the general approach to environmental problems was changing and the Community introduced new instruments to modernise its action. The Treaty as amended in 1987, and the 1992 Maastricht Treaty, proclaimed the integration of environmental protection into the Community's other policies. Also in 1992, the 5th Action Programme entitled 'Towards Sustainability' was adopted. It provides for the implementation of fiscal, economic and financial instruments and opens up channels of information, communication, education and consultation. Today, more than ever, the Community needs dialogue, cooperation and partnership with national, regional and local authorities, with social and economic agents, associations and citizens, so that everyone can be involved in safeguarding our environment and natural resources.

Nevertheless, legislation remains an important instrument. In several of the spheres in which the European Union is competent, by virtue of the principle of subsidiarity, environmental assessment leads to the introduction of new legislation — as does the carrying out of international obligations.

So it is still very useful to publish these volumes of *Community legislation on the environment*. The first edition was in 1993, and this second edition is the first update. As before, it is being published in all the official languages of the European Union, for use by the growing number of individuals responsible for environmental issues within governments, industry, educational establishments and private organisations. It is hoped that these volumes will provide a useful tool for all those wishing to be involved in the vital task of protecting the environment, safeguarding natural resources and promoting sustainable development.

Ritt Bjerregaard,
Member of the Commission

General introduction

Environment protection in the framework of the Community law

In accordance with the original intentions of the founders, the European Community has developed into a supranational government which — as it approaches its 40th year — is in the process of increasing its membership, thus deepening its democratic structure and strengthening its powers.

Six European states (Belgium, France, Italy, Luxembourg, the Netherlands and the Federal Republic of Germany) — determined to lay the foundations of an ever closer union among the peoples[1] of Europe — joined together on 1 January 1958 to create the European Economic Community[2]. Denmark, the United Kingdom and Ireland joined in 1973, Greece in 1981, and Spain and Portugal in 1985. Finally, in 1995, Austria, Finland and Sweden brought EC Membership to fifteen countries. Today, the list of countries which have declared their intention to seek membership in the European Community would include most of Europe, especially the Central European States which see close ties to the community as a crucial source of economic growth and democratic stability.

Where early post-war proposals for European union failed, Jean Monnet and French Foreign Minister Robert Schuman's pragmatic approach succeeded. 'A united Europe will not emerge overnight or in one grand design. It will be built on practical achievements, creating first a *de facto* interdependence.' Schuman declared.

---

[1] Preamble to the Treaty establishing the European Economic Community, Treaties establishing the European Communities, Office for Official Publications of the European Communities (Luxembourg : 1987), p 217. References in the text to the Treaty mean the EEC Treaty. The EEC Treaty together with the 1951 Treaty establishing the European Coal and Steel Community and the 1957 Treaty establishing the European Atomic Energy Community make up the Constitution of the European Community.

[2] The European Parliament resolved to use the term 'European Community' in 1975 to refer to the supranational political entity created by the founding Treaties. This term is increasingly used in Community documents, e.g. in Article 130r which refers to 'action by the Community relating to the environment'. However, while it is an appropriate designation for the political entity, it occasionally comes into conflict with legal texts under the Treaties, each of which established a separate 'Community', and in formal references to the Community institutions. For example, the formal title of the Commission is : 'Commission of the European Communities', meaning that it is the sole executive authority for the three founding Treaties.

From the outset, the Member States delegated powers to the Community to legislate, implement and enforce the Community's legislation that went beyond the powers of any other international organisation.

The EC is characterised by a number of features which make it unique:

1) legislative, executive and judicial organs of government;
2) a transfer of powers from the Member States to the Community by virtue of treaties;
3) supremacy of Community law over national law, which is subject to exclusive review by the Community's Court of Justice.

Two milestones on the road to a united Europe were the agreement in 1967 to merge the separate organs of government of the three founding treaties which together provide the Community's constitutional framework, and the 1976 Act introducing the direct election of the members of the European Parliament[1].

Another major step forward came on 1 July 1987 when the Single European Act amending the Treaties came into effect[2]. The Single European Act reiterates the objective of economic and monetary union formally declared by the Heads of State at the 1972 Paris Summit, amends and completes the Founding Treaties and contains provisions which codify principles of political cooperation, in particular the endeavour 'to jointly formulate and implement a European foreign policy'[3].

These amendments introduced the aim of achieving an internal market without national frontiers before 31 December 1992. They also introduced for the first time two explicit references to the Community's powers concerning environmental protection: Article 100a stipulates the criteria for environmental protection legislation affecting the internal market and allows legislation to be adopted by qualified majority in the Council. Articles 130r, 130s and 130t lay down the objectives, means and procedures for the adoption of legislation regarding the environment, specifying, however, that these decisions must be taken unanimously.

The Treaty of the European Union, which was signed by the Heads of State and Government of the European Community Member States in Maastricht on 7 February 1992 and which must be ratified by the Member States in 1992, extended the application of the cooperation procedure to environmental legislation generally under Articles 130s. Unanimity is still required in three areas:

---

[1] Act concerning the election of the representatives of the European Parliament by direct universal suffrage, annexed to Council Decision 76/787/ECSC, EEC, EURATOM (OJ L 278, 8.10.1976).

[2] Single European Act (OJ L 169, 29.6.1987, p. 1).

[3] Article 30 (1).

- provisions primarily of a fiscal nature;

- measures concerning town and country planning, land use with the exception of waste management, measures of a general nature and the management of water resources; and

- measures significantly affecting a Member State's choice between different energy sources and the general structure of its energy supply.

The EC's powers regarding the environment

The European Community is an institution with limited powers delegated to it through the Treaties defining both the areas of the Community's exclusive power and the areas where the Community and the Member States jointly decide. Other areas are by definition the competence of the Member States. The environment is one of the areas in which competence is shared and the area of external relations is another. Member States are thus free to adopt legislation in the absence of Community legislation, but where the Community has acted, Community legislation is supreme and binding on both past and future Member State actions.

The European Community can and does actively participate in the preparation of international conventions on the environment and in their implementation. In addition, the Court of Justice has upheld the direct effect of international agreements to which the Community is a part[1] Community regulations, decisions and directives must be enforced in national courts if the obligation at issue is expressed in a sufficiently precise and unconditional manner.

Types of Community legislation

The European Community can adopt:

- Non-binding **recommendations** and **resolutions**;

- **Regulations** that are binding and directly applicable in all Member States;

- **Decisions** that are directly binding on the persons to whom they are addressed, including Member States, individuals and legal persons.

- **Directives** which must be implemented by the national laws or regulations of the Member States within a designated time limit (normally 18 months to two years).

---

[1]   Case 87/75 Bresciani, [1976] ECR 129.

For more than 20 years, the Directive was the main tool of the Community's environmental policy. The Community defines objectives, standards and procedures allowing the Member States some flexibility in integrating them into their national systems of administration and law. Thus, where one Member State may choose to enact a new law virtually reproducing the text of the Directive, another Member State which already has legislation in the sector covered by the Directive may choose to implement it by amending the previous law or by means of administrative regulations.

Because it sometimes takes years to fully implement directives and Member States may differ concerning the transformation of the directives into national law, the Community has recently turned to the adoption of regulations because of their taking effect more rapidly and applying directly throughout the Community.

The EEC Treaty establishes different requirements for the entry into force of each type of Community legislation:

- Regulations must take effect on the date specified in them or, failing that, on the twentieth day following their publication in the Official Journal of the European Communities.

- Directives and decisions must be notified to those they are addressed to and take effect upon their notification. The notification dates are indicated in the footnotes. Directives often give a deadline by which the Member State must have implemented them.

- International treaties take effect when they have been ratified by a certain number of countries. The dates on which these treaties took effect in the Community are indicated in the footnotes.

The institutions of the European Community

The main institutions of the EC include:

- the directly elected **European Parliament**;

- the **Council of Ministers** which has the fundamental power to adopt legislation;

- the **Commission of the European Communities** which has the sole power to propose legislation and which also implements and enforces it; and

- the **Court of Justice** which assures that Community law and the treaties are respected.

The Commission

The European Commission is the executive organ of the European Community. It consists of 20 Commissioners proposed by the Member States and serving a collective 5-year term of office. It employs about 15,000 civil servants. All must swear allegiance to the European Community and declare that they are free from influence by their national governments. Only the Commission has the power to propose legislation. Before doing so, it generally consults with experts from the Member States, from industry and from the groups concerned. Its proposals are published in the *Official Journal of the European Communities*.

Moreover, the Commission is also responsible for implementing, monitoring and controlling the enforcement of Community law and policy. In this respect, it may well bring a Member State before the Court of Justice for not complying with Community law. Finally, it administers the Community budget.

In certain specific cases, the Council can in addition authorise the Commission to adopt complementary legal texts to assure the Community legislation's implementation. This power is generally used to amend the technical Annexes to the original legislation. The Member States participate in the process through one of a series of procedures laid down in Council Decision 87/373/EEC[1].

The Commission consists of 23 Directorates-general, a legal service and a general secretariat. Directorate-General XI (DG-XI) is responsible for environment, nuclear safety and civil protection. Worker protection, industrial technical regulation, regional development and aid to third countries are the responsibility of other DGs. Support for the DGs is provided by a number of other specialised services of the Commission.

The role of the Commission in the law-making process regarding the environment has become increasingly important over the years. Member States must notify the Commission before adopting any legislation that could possibly affect the common market, including most of the environmental legislation aimed at industry and which gives the Community the possibility to adopt Community-wide measures[2]. When the environment is concerned, it is increasingly common for a Member State to take the lead and for other Member States to turn to the Commission to work out a proposal to harmonise the environmental standards within this sector in all Member States rather than adopting their own national policy.

---

[1] Council Decision 87/373/EEC of 13 July 1987 laying down the procedures for the exercise of implementing powers conferred on the Commission (OJ L 197, 18.7.1987, p. 33).

The Commission also plays an increasing important role in international environmental policy-making. For example, it participates in the work of the Organisation for Economic Cooperation and Development (OECD) and regularly receives mandates from the Council for the negotiation of international treaties on the environment. The European Environmental Agency and its environmental information and observation network were established by the Council to provide the Community, the Member States and other European countries with reliable and comparable information to enable them to take the necessary measures to protect the quality of the environment. The Commission also manages the budget allocated by the Community for aid to Central and Eastern Europe (PHARE) and has been given the task of coordinating all of the aid programmes of the G-24 (OECD) countries.

Once legislation has been adopted, the Commission's fundamental task is to ensure that it is correctly applied by the Member States, formally as well as in practice.

Environmental legislation often provides the Commission with responsibilities that go beyond its duty to monitor and control, for example the development and management of an information system, the defining of guidelines, the organization of technical training, etc. The Commission also convenes regular meetings in Brussels of the national authorities responsible for the implementation of environmental legislation in order to discuss practical problems arising during the implementation of the legislation, needs of information and education or the amendment or adaptation of the legislation to scientific and technical developments.

---

[2] Council Directive 83/189/EEC of 28 March 1983, laying down a procedure for the provision of information in the field of technical standards and regulations (standstill) (OJ L 109,26.4.1983, p. 8). This Directive stipulates that Member States should notify the Commission well in advance about the adoption of measures liable to affect the Community's or the Member States' policy or the workings of the internal market so as to enable the Commission to propose a harmonised legislation dealing with the subject in question. The Directive 83/189/EEC includes a procedure for Member states to follow in case of creating national standards or technical regulations liable to affect the Common Market by creating non-tariff trade barriers. A large number of national environmental measures is included in this Directive for they impose regulations or define standards applicable to either the process of industrial production or the products, implying a direct or indirect impact on industry and trade.

The Council

The Council is the main legislative organ of the Community and represents the interests of the Member States. It is composed of one representative from each of the governments of the Member States, generally at ministerial level. The foreign affairs minister usually represents the Member State on general matters. The 'Environmental Council' is composed of the ministers responsible for the environment. The presidency of the Council passes from one Member State to another every six months according to an order defined unanimously by the Council. The Member States maintain a permanent representation in Brussels.

The Council is assisted by a standing Committee of Permanent Representations (COREPER) who carry out the day-to-day political work preceding agreements and a Committee of the Regions for consultation.

The European Parliament

The European Parliament represents the interests of the citizens of the European Community but has neither the power to propose legislation nor to adopt it. It does, however, have the power to approve the budget and to dismiss the Commission. Nevertheless, its role has steadily gained importance over the years. The Treaty of the European Union has significantly increased, its powers no longer being merely consultative and controlling. From now on it will exercise " the powers attributed by the present Treaty"[1].

The European Parliament participates in the process of adopting Community Acts both by exercising its powers within the framework of the procedures defined in Articles 189 B and 189 C and by giving either confirming or consultative opinions.

Moreover, it has acquired an official role in the adopted legislation by virtue of the procedures of cooperation and co-decision introduced by the Single European Act and by the Treaty of the European Union respectively. This procedure of cooperation applies, by virtue of Article 130 S (1) of the Treaty, to the actions undertaken by the Community in order to bring about the objectives put forward by the Community's environmental policy.

Members of the European Parliament are elected every five years and are divided into political groups organized at community level.

The Parliament meets for one week a month, usually in Strasbourg (France). Its sessions are open to the public. The commissions usually meet in the pre-

---

[1]   Article 137.

ceding week in Brussels. Many commission meetings are open to the public, including those of the Environment, Public Health and Consumer Affairs Commissions.

The legislative procedures

Under the **consultation procedure**, the Commission must send its proposals to the Council, which is usually required to request the opinions of the European Parliament and the Economic and Social Committee. After counselling the European Parliament and the Economic and Social Committee, the proposal is returned to the Council where it will be examined by the COREPER working group concerned. Once the report of this working group has been drawn up, the proposal is studied by COREPER and is then returned to the Council. When COREPER reaches an agreement concerning the Commission's proposal, it is entered into the Council's agenda as item A. Item As are generally adopted by the Council without preliminary discussion. When, on the other hand, no consensus can be reached, the proposal is entered in the Council's agenda as item B implying that the proposal needs to be discussed and negotiated before it is voted or amended by the Council. Whether a simple majority, qualified majority or unanimity is needed depends on the authorizing provision on which the proposal is based.

If the Council is unable to adopt the proposal in accordance with the voting system mentioned in the provision concerned, the proposal is not completely overruled but is merely suspended or, as is increasingly the case, amended or withdrawn by the Commission. Occasionally, an appeal is made to the Council to resolve the deadlock.

This type of consultation applies to the environmental legislation for:

- Provisions primarily of a fiscal nature;

- measures concerning town and country planning, land use with the exception of waste management, measures of a general nature and the management of water resources;

- measures significantly affecting a Member State's choice between different energy sources and the general structure of its energy supply.

The **cooperation procedure** *(figure 1)* was introduced through the Single European Act in order to accomplish two objectives: on the one hand, it was meant to strengthen the role of the Parliament in the law-making process and, on the other hand, to accelerate the legislative process, requiring the Council to adopt a large number of acts by qualified majority and imposing deadlines on the present phase of the procedure's cooperation.

The cooperation procedure also stipulates that the Commission must send its proposals to the Council, which again is obliged to counsel the European Parliament and the Economic and Social Committee. Upon receiving the Parliament's opinion, the Council agrees a common position which is sent back to the Parliament for a second reading. Within three months following this transmission, the European Parliament may approve the common position, not pronounce its opinion, reject it by absolute majority of the constituent members or propose amendments to the Council's common position by the same majority.

If one of the two first-mentioned alternatives is chosen by the Parliament, the Council decides upon the act in accordance with its common position. If the act is rejected, however, the Council can only decide by unanimity. Finally, when the European Parliament opts for to amend the text of the common position, the Commission has three months to re-examine the proposal it based its common position on, starting from the amendments proposed by the European Parliament. Afterwards, the Commission sends not only its re-examined proposal to the Council but also the amendments that have not been accepted, together with the Commission's opinion on them. The Council can adopt these amendments by unanimity and enact the Commission's re-examined proposal by qualified majority of its members. It can also modify the Commission's re-examined proposal by unanimity. The Council is required to decide within three months. If no decision has come through by that time, the proposal is considered not-adopted.

The Treaty of the European Union has significantly enlarged the application of this legislative procedure. Within the framework of the environmental policy, actions to be undertaken by the Community to bring about the objectives mentioned in Article 130R will be decided upon according to the cooperation procedure defined in Article 189c of the Treaty.

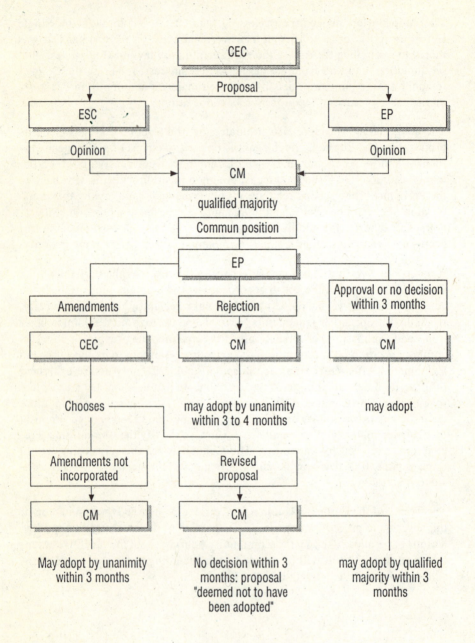

The **co-decision procedure** *(figure 2)* was first introduced by the Treaty of the European Union. This procedure allows the European Parliament to amend or to use its veto regarding certain acts of the Council. Thus, the Parliament is certain to play a more active role in the adoption of Community Legislation. Article 189 B of the Treaty describes the way in which the Parliament exercises its power of co-decision.

Upon submission of a Commission's proposal to the Council and the Parliament, the Council adopts a common position by qualified majority after counselling the Parliament. This common position is subsequently transmitted to the European Parliament. Within a period of three months after this transmission, the European Parliament may approve the common position, not pronounce its opinion, reject it by absolute majority of its constituent members or propose amendments to the common position by the same majority.

If one of the two first-mentioned alternatives is chosen by the Parliament, the Council decides upon the act in accordance with its common position. If the Parliament intends to reject the common position, it is required to inform the Council immediately. The Council can subsequently make an appeal to the Conciliation Committee[1] to fine-tune its position. Subsequently, the European Parliament either confirms the rejection of the common position by absolute majority of its constituent members implying that the act will not be adopted, or proposes amendments. Amendments to the common position need the Parliament's absolute majority of its members after which the amended text is transmitted to the Council and the Commission which have to reach an opinion on it.

If the Council approves the Parliament's amendments by qualified majority within three months, it consequently modifies its position and decrees the act concerned.

If the Council does not decree the act concerned, a meeting of the Conciliation Committee is convened. The Conciliation Committee must reach an agreement on a common project by qualified majority of its members. The Conciliation Committee must approve a common project within six weeks following its convocation. In this case, the Parliament, having decided by absolute majority and the Council, having decided by qualified majority, have another six weeks upon this approval to decree the act concerned in accordance with the common project. If one of the two institutions fails to approve the common project, the act is considered not-adopted which is also the result if the Conciliation Committee has not been able to agree on a common project. However, during the second six-week period starting immediately after the expiry of the six weeks

---

[1] The Committee of Reconciliation consists of the members of the Council or their representatives and an equal number of representatives of the European Parliament.

granted to the Conciliation Committee, the Council may confirm, by qualified majority, the common position it had agreed upon before the procedure of reconciliation was initiated. This confirmation may possibly include the amendments put forward by the European Parliament. In this case, the act concerned is finally decreed but the European Parliament always has the final word enabling it to reject the text by absolute majority of its members within six weeks following the Council's confirmation, thus causing the act to be considered not-adopted.

Article 130S (3) of the Treaty enables the co-decision procedure to be applicable to the Council's decisions concerning decreeing general action programmes concentrating on environmental priority objectives. The measures needed to implement these programmes are agreed upon according to the procedure of consultation or cooperation, depending on the case.

The legislative procedure also implies numerous direct consultations with the national governments through COREPER and private organisations, both at national and community level. Before expressing their stances regarding proposals for Community legislation, Member States often officially consult their national parliaments and proceed with informally consulting national interest groups.

This complicated consultation process is absolutely necessary to draw up a legislation to:

- assure a 'high level of protection' of public health and the environment;
- harmonise industrial standards and procedures Community-wide;
- be integrated in the various legal systems of the Member States; and
- be implemented by the various administrations and by the various levels of government.

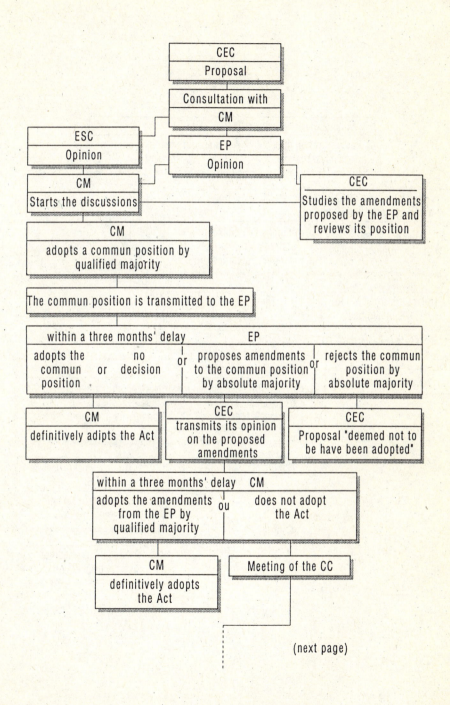

CEC
Proposal

Consultation with
CM

ESC
Opinion

EP
Opinion

CM
Starts the discussions

CEC
Studies the amendments
proposed by the EP and
reviews its position

CM
adopts a commun position by
qualified majority

The commun position is transmitted to the EP

within a three months' delay   EP

adopts the   no   or   proposes amendments   or   rejects the commun
commun   or   decision   to the commun position   position by
position   by absolute majority   absolute majority

CM
definitively adipts the Act

CEC
transmits its opinion
on the proposed
amendments

CEC
Proposal "deemed not to
be have been adopted"

within a three months' delay   CM

adopts the amendments   ou   does not adopt
from the EP by   the Act
qualified majority

CM
definitively adopts
the Act

Meeting of the CC

(next page)

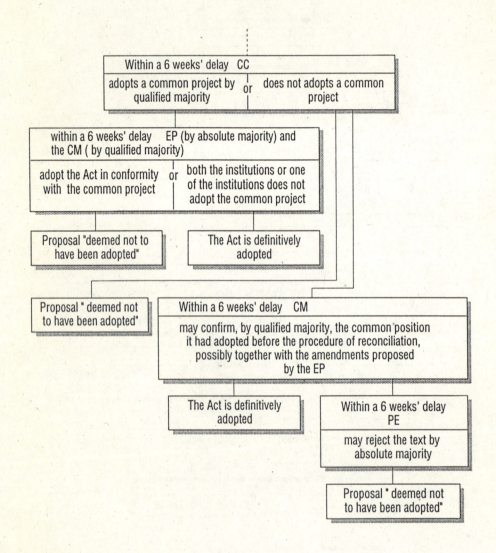

The Court of justice

The Court of Justice is the guardian of the Treaties of Community law. It is composed of judges appointed by agreement with the Member States. The judges are assisted by advocates general, who analyse and propose decisions on the cases before it.

Cases may be brought by the Community institutions against each other, by the Commission against a Member State or vice versa. Cases may also be brought by natural or legal persons against Member States or the Commission under Community law.

Regarding the Court of Justice, the major change introduced by the Treaty of the European Union, is the power granted to the Court to impose fines on Member States[1]. When a Member State fails to take the measures included in the execution of a decree established by the Court of Justice, the Commission may go to Court. The Commission determines the amount of the fine or the penalty to be paid by the Member State, taking into consideration the circumstances. If the Court of Justice finds that a Member State is not complying with its decree, it may impose the payment of the fine or the penalty.

The national courts have the power to review actions taken by their governments for the implementation and enforcement of Community legislation. They may apply to the Court of Justice for a preliminary ruling on an issue of EC law before taking a decision. Moreover, national courts have the power to enforce the decisions of the Court of Justice.

The Court of Justice has rarely ruled on the substance of Community environmental law but several decisions are of fundamental importance in defining the power of the Community to limit the lawmaking authority of the Member States.

The principle of the direct applicability of Community law to individuals was first enunciated in 1963, when the Court stated: 'The Community constitutes a new legal order of international law for the benefit of which the States have limited their sovereign rights, albeit within limited fields", and 'independently of the legislation of Member States, Community law not only imposes obligations on individuals but is intended to confer upon them rights which become part of their legal heritage. These rights arise not only where they are expressly granted by the Treaty but also by reason of obligations which the Treaty imposes in a clearly defined way upon individuals as well as upon the Member States and upon the institutions of the Community"[2].

---

[1] Article 171 (2).

[2] Case 26/62 Van Gend & Loos [1963] ECR 10 ; Case 8/81 Becker vs Finanzamt Münster [1982] ECR 50 ; see also Jean-Victor Luis, The Community Legal Order, 2nd ed., Office for Official Publications of the European Community (Luxembourg : 1990).

Hence, in spite of the fact that a Member State has not implemented (or not properly implemented) a Community environmental directive in violation of Article 189 (13) of the Treaty, the Directive may take direct effect. However, the provisions of the Directive regarding the obligations of the Member State must be sufficiently precise and unconditional in order to have the direct effect of national law vis-à-vis the citizen[1]. They must also be capable of being enforced as law by the national courts.

A landmark environmental ruling came in September 1988 when the Court upheld a Danish law requiring all beer and soft drinks to be sold in reusable containers with a deposit. The ensuing trade barrier to non-resident producers (which for reasons of weight and cost prefer to use throw-away containers) was justified because of the 'imperative requirement' to protect the environment in the absence of a Community law covering this issue. The Court nevertheless struck down a clause of the Danish law which limits the quantity of beverages that non-resident manufacturers may import in bottles that do not conform to Danish standards taking the view that this was a significant trade barrier insofar as Danish exporters faced no similar restrictions in other Member States[2].

Evolution of EC Environmental protection policies

In the 1950s, European politicians sought to rebuild European prosperity and secure peace in the future by creating a common trading area. The core objective of the 1957 Treaty of Rome, establishing the European Economic Community, was 'the constant improvement in the living and working conditions' of the European peoples.

Protection of the environment as such did not appear in the EEC Treaty. However, not so many years later, Community lawmakers recognised the need to create common standards to protect consumers in order to assure the free circulation of goods among the Member States. Thus, the first Community environmental legislation dealt with products (dangerous chemicals, motor vehicles and detergents). Product and later industry-related environmental legislation was based on Article 100 of the Treaty, which covered the harmonisation of laws 'in Member States as having a direct impact on the establishment or functioning of the common market.' In addition, environmental legislation was based on Article 235, covering measures which 'prove necessary to attain... one of the objectives of the Community' in the absence of a specific

---

[1] Ludwig Krämer, 'Effet national des directives communautaires en matière d'environnement', 1990 RJE 3, pp. 325 — 349.

[2] Case 302/86 Commission vs Denmark [1988] ECR 4607.

delegation of power by the Treaty. Until 1987, all Community environmental legislation was based upon one or the other or both of these Articles.

In the late 1960s, it became obvious that drastic and comprehensive measures would be needed to protect the Community's environment from the demands imposed on it by economic growth. By the end of the 1970s, the global dimensions of environmental pollution were becoming apparent. In 1972 (the year of the first United Nations conference on the environment), the European Community adopted its first five-year environmental action programme (1973 — 1977) setting out the principles and priorities that would guide its policies in the future.

The first and second environmental action programmes[1] set out detailed lists of actions to be taken to control a broad range of pollution problems. Eleven principles were listed, which have remained valid in subsequent action programmes[2]:

1)   Prevention is better than cure. This principle has become paramount under the fourth environmental action programme.

2)   Environmental impacts should be taken into account at the earliest possible stage in decision-making.

3)   Any form of exploitation of resources and of the natural environment which causes significant damage to the ecological balance must be avoided.

4)   Scientific knowledge must be improved to enable efficient action to be taken in this field.

5)   The 'Polluter pays' principle: that is, the cost of preventing and repairing environmental damage should be borne by the polluter.

6)   Activities in one Member State should not cause deterioration of the environment in another.

7)   Environmental policy in the Member States must take into account the interests of the developing countries.

8)   The EC and its Member States should promote international and world-wide environmental protection through international organisations.

9)   Environmental protection is everyone's responsibility, therefore education is necessary.

---

[1]   OJ C 112, 20.12.1973, p. 1 ; OJ C 139, 13.6.1977, p. 1.
[2]   A number of these principles have been reiterated in Articles 100a and 130r, 130s and 130t of the Treaty.

10) Environmental protection measures should be taken at the most 'appropriate level', taking into account the type of pollution, the action needed and the geographical zone to be protected. This is known as the "subsidiary principle".

11) National environmental programmes should be coordinated on the basis of a common long-term concept and national policies should be harmonised within the Community, not in isolation.

The third environmental action programme, adopted in 1983[1], tried to provide an overall strategy for the protection of the environment and natural resources in the European Community. It shifted the emphasis from pollution control to pollution prevention, and broadened the concept of environmental protection to include land use planning and the integration of environmental concerns into the other EC policies. The areas affected include the funds for agricultural activities, regional economic development, and aid to African, Caribbean and Pacific countries within the framework of the Lomé Convention.

The fourth environmental action programme[2] (1987 — 1992) sought in part to give substance to the new obligations for integration of the environmental dimension into other Community policies by emphasising four areas of activity:

1) Effective and complete implementation of existing Community Legislation;

2) Regulation of all environmental impacts of 'substances' and 'sources' of pollution;

3) Increased public access to and dissemination of information;

4) Job creation.

The fifth environmental action programme[3] (1993 — 2000) signifies a watershed for the Community. As in the 1980s the major challenge consisted in bringing about the internal market, in the present decade it consists of the reconciliation between environment and development.

In order to achieve tangible results in this respect within the time limit of the fifth programme, the following fields of action have priority:

---

[1] OJ C 46, 17.2.1983, p. 1.
[2] OJ C 328, 1987, p.1.
[3] OJ C 138, 17.5.1993, p .1.

1) Long-term management of natural resources: soil, water, nature reserves and coastal areas.

2) The overall fight against pollution and preventive action concerning waste.

3) Reducing the consumption of non-renewable energy sources.

4) Improving mobility management, notably by opting for more efficient and environmental-friendly locations and means of transport.

5) Health and security improvements, particularly regarding the assessment and management of industrial hazards, nuclear safety and protection against radiation.

Tackling these challenges implies adopting new strategies which aim at breaking the tendencies set out by preceding action programmes and turning towards long-term development.

These strategies imply an active commitment of all the major participants and provide access to a wider range of resources including, notably, economic instruments and the improvement of information aimed at contributing to the identifiable and measurable environmental improvements or aim at changing consumer habits which is the principal source of our planet's deterioration.

The Single European Act

The amendments to the Treaty of Rome, which took effect on 1 July 1987, introduced a series of new articles on the environment in the third part of the Treaty which covers the 'foundation and policy of the Community'. Three articles (130r, 130s and 130t) set out the objectives and elements of environmental protection actions by the Community. The objectives of this action are defined as follows:

- to preserve, protect and improve the quality of the environment;

- to contribute towards protecting human health,

- to assure a prudent and rational utilisation of natural resources.

EC environmental protection actions must become integrated into other EC policies, the most important of which are agriculture, regional development and energy and must be based on three principles:

- preventive action;

- environmental damage must be rectified at source;

- the polluter pays.

The integration principle is by far the most significant provision in the new article. Environmental protection is the only area of EC policy that imposes such a sweeping requirement; and the Community must adopt procedures to implement and enforce it[1].

Article 130s stipulates the requirement of unanimity on the Council[2]. However, the Commission and the Court of Justice have made it clear that Community environmental legislation sets minimum standards, but may not be used to prevent the Member States from going further: 'The protective measures adopted in common pursuant to Article 130s shall not prevent any Member State from introducing more stringent protective measures compatible with this Treaty[3].'

The Single European Act recognised the complicated relationship between the environment and trade in a new Article 100a which states that when the Commission proposes a law concerning health, safety, environmental protection and consumer protection affecting the common market, that proposal must 'take as a base a high level of protection'. Again, Member States are given the opportunity to adopt more stringent standards if they deem it necessary.

The cooperation procedure under Article 100a was first used to break the deadlock on emission limits for medium and large-engine motor vehicles. In April 1987, the Parliament amended the Council text to impose stricter controls on emissions from small-engine cars and managed to convince the Commission to introduce the same standards instead. The Council was forced to agree.

In June 1991, the Court of Justice issued a judgement[4] regarding the legal basis of Directive 89/428/EEC on a progressive phase-out programme for the disposal of titanium dioxide wastes. Through this judgement, the Court cleared the way for the Community to adopt environmental legislation affecting industry by qualified majority instead of unanimity.

The Commission based its proposed Directive on Article 100a of the Treaty (measures furthering the single market) but the Council disagreed and opted for Article 130s on the environment.

---

[1] Pascale Kromarek, 'The Single European Act and the Environment', in European Environment Review 1, 1986, pp. 10 — 12.

[2] It also allows the Council to define matters on which decisions will be taken by majority opinion.

[3] Article 130t.

[4] Case 300/89 Commission vs Council [1991].

Under Article 100a, the European Parliament would have two readings of a proposal which could be adopted by qualified majority. In practice, basing legislation on Article 100a gives the more environmentally progressive forces in Parliament and the Council greater influence over the final text, but this practice has been strongly fought against by some Member States which are concerned about the Parliament's increased power and the loss of national legislative authority to the Community.

Under the terms of Article 130s, the Parliament has only one "consultative" reading and the Council must decide by unanimity (which is sometimes difficult to achieve).

The Court struck down the Directive, accepting the Commission's argument that since national environmental laws regulating this industry could lead to distortions in competition, Article 100a was the correct legal basis for creating a harmonised Community system. Since Article 100a (3) states that such laws affecting the environment must achieve 'a high level of protection', it is clear that, according to the Court, 'the objectives of environmental protection cited in Article 130r can be efficiently pursued through harmonisation measures based on Article 100a'.

This decision cleared up a knotty problem that had been pending since July 1987 when the amendments to the Treaty took effect. It means that the Commission is free to base other environmental proposals on Article 100a without fear of upset in the Council.

The Treaty of the European Union

The Treaty of the European Union significantly modifies the 'environment' sector of the EEC Treaty adding a fourth objective of the environmental policy to Article 130r. Community policy should 'contribute to promoting on an international scale measures taken to deal with regional or global environmental problems.'

Concerning the environment, the Treaty also implies a policy of high-level protection, taking into account the diversity of the Community's regions.

The new Article 130r (2) strengthens the existing provision that environmental needs must be integrated in the definition and implementation of all other Community policies. Measures of harmonisation dealing with these needs may include a safeguard clause, authorising Member States to take temporary measures based on non-economic environmental reasons, under a Community procedure of supervision.

The Treaty deletes the fourth paragraph of Article 130r which stipulates that "the Community acts in environmental matters whose objectives can easier be achieved at Community level than at national level". Nevertheless, the environmental policy generally remains submitted to the subsidiary principle in Article 3 B of the Treaty. It also stipulates that Decisions are to be made as close to citizen-level as possible[1].

Article 130s stipulates that concerning its contents, the Council must decide by qualified majority[2] in accordance with the procedure of cooperation determined in Article 189c in order to attain the objectives stipulated in Article 130r. Unanimity, however, is required for:

- provisions primarily of a fiscal nature;

- measures concerning town and country planning, land use with the exception of waste management, measures of a general nature and the management of water resources;

- measures significantly affecting the choice of a Member State between different energy sources and the general structure of its energy supply.

Action programmes of a general nature regarding priority objectives are adopted by the Council in accordance with the cooperation procedure established in Article 189 B of the Treaty.

The Member States have to assure the funding and execution of the Community's environmental policy. If the policy's implementation implies funds going beyond the Member State's means, the Council includes in the act containing the measure taken in order to achieve the objectives set out in Article 130r (1) the appropriate provisions by means of a temporary derogation and/or financial support from the Cohesion Fund.

Financial instruments for the environment

On 26 May 1994, the Cohesion fund[3] replaced the financial instrument of cohesion[4], introducing a financial backing to both environmental projects and transeuropean networks of transport in the Member States whose Gross

---

[1] Article A.
[2] The Council is authorised by Article 130s to determine the matters to be voted by qualified majority.
[3] The Council's Regulation (EEC) 1164/94 from 16 May 1994 establishing the Cohesion Fund (OJ L 130,25.05.1994, p.1).
[4] The Council's Regulation (EEC) 792/93 from 30 March 1993 establishing a funding instrument of cohesion (OJ L 97, 01.04.1993, p. 74).

National Product per capita is less than 90% of the Community's average: i.e. Greece, Spain, Portugal and Ireland.

In order to be eligible, environmental projects must contribute to the completion of the objectives mentioned in Article 130r of the Treaty, including the measures taken in conformity with Article 130s and the objectives which have priority within the Community's environmental policy. A project's funding by the Cohesion Fund is agreed upon by the Commission consonant with the Member State in question. The funding rate is between 80 and 85% of public spending and is in line with the interventions to be made. In order to make sure that the projects financed by the Cohesion Fund are correctly carried out and in order to avoid any irregularity whatsoever, a control system was introduced by the Member States.

The financial instrument for the environment (Life) introduces a financial backing to actions contributing to the implementation of the Community's environmental policy based on the principle of "the polluter pays". Also eligible are projects of technical support to third countries around the Mediterranean and the Baltic sea and, more exceptionally, to regional and global actions regarding environmental problems as established international agreements.

Financial backing is either agreed upon as co-financing, the level of which varies between 30 and 100% according to the kind of action or as an interest reduction.

Proposals of actions to be financed must be submitted to the Commission by the Member State concerned. These proposals are then studied by a committee made up of representatives from the Member States and the Commission and are adopted, in most cases, by the Commission.

The Commission is also responsible for the success of the projects financially supported by the Community. If any irregularities are found, it has the right to decrease, suspend or reclaim the funds awarded.

Communication 94/C 139/03[1] defines the priority actions to be implemented in 1995 within the framework of LIFE.

Finally, the new provisions included in the modified regulations concerning the Structural Funds, adopted in July 1993[2], increased the attention given to

---

[1]   The Commission's communication 94/C 139/03 in conformity with the Council's regulation (EEC) 1973/92 containing the creation of a funding instrument for the environment (Life) regarding the priority actions to be carried out in 1995 (OJ C 139, 21.05.1994, p. 3).

[2]   OJ L 215, 30.07.1992, p. 85.

environmental problems. These provisions want these national and regional funding programmes to bring about a revaluation of the national and regional environmental situation as well as the results of the actions aimed at. It also specifies that these programmes must specify the provisions agreed upon with the authorities concerned.

Citizen rights under Community Law

The Treaty of the European Union introduces a European citizenship. "Every person with the nationality of a Member State is a citizen of the Union'.

Citizens of the Union have five general rights:

1) The right to travel and reside unconditionally on the territory of a Member State;

2) The right to vote as well as the eligibility in both municipal elections and elections for the European Parliament in the Member State in which they reside under the same conditions as the nationals;

3) The right to protection from the diplomatic and consular authorities of every Member State on the territory of a third country where his country is not represented;

4) The right to petition the European Parliament about a matter within the Community's competence which directly concerns him; and

5) The right to complain to the ombudsman, appointed by the European Parliament, regarding wrong administration of the Community's institutions or organs except for the Court of Justice and the Court of First Instance concerning the exercise of their judicial powers.

In addition to these rights directly related to Union citizenship, citizens also have the right to formally complain to the Commission about a violation of Community law; this may form the basis of an infringement proceeding by the Commission against the Member State concerned.

European citizens only have the right to bring a complaint directly before the Court of Justice under decisions or regulations addressed directly and individually to them. Since directives are addressed to the Member States, no standing arises for citizens or citizen groups. However, citizen groups have the right to appear before the Court of Justice in support of a case already before the Court, if the Court agrees that the group has a legal interest in supporting the case (e.g. a consumer organisation in a consumer protection case).

Introduction

None of the sectors under the Community environmental policy is governed by so vast a body of legislation as is water, particularly where the fight against pollution is concerned. Since the start of the 1970s, more than forty texts on the subject (Regulations, Directives, Decisions....) have been adopted. The issue fuelling the debate has always been: do we have to establish quality standards for water or do we have to impose emission standards for water pollutants

The quality standards define the desired quality of the environment whereby the introduction of certain pollutants is tolerated, while the emission standards set maximum quantities for the pollutants which can be emitted and are thus stricter than the former. In the end, the result is an environmental policy based on a "parallel approach". While it gives priority to establishing emission standards, the Community legislation on pollution of the aquatic environment does not discard the implementation of quality objectives which the waters must meet.

The emission of dangerous substances in surface waters

Directive 76/464/EEC[1] aims at eliminating the pollution of the Community's surface waters, territorial waters, coastal waters, groundwater by the substances mentioned in List I of the Annexe and the reduction of their pollution by the substances in List II of the Annexe. List I contains the most dangerous substances with regard to their toxicity, persistence and bio-accumulation. List II contains the substances having a limited harmful effect on the aquatic environment.

The substances mentioned in List I may not be emitted into the water without an authorisation. This authorisation is required to contain emission values which limit the maximum concentration of a substance in the emissions. These values may at the very most be as strict as the restrictions imposed on the emission of substances mentioned in List I adopted by the Council and must be limited in time. As regards the substances mentioned in List II, the Member States define the programmes designed to reduce water pollution. These pro-

---

[1]   Council Directive 76/464/EEC, of 4 May 1976, on pollution caused by certain dangerous substances discharged into the aquatic environment of the Community (OJ L 129; 18.05.1976, p. 23). See also Community Legislation concerning the environment, Volume 7, Water, first edition, p. 47 and xxx.

grammes not only contain quality objectives for water but possibly also specific provisions regarding the composition and use of dangerous substances and products. Moreover, they take into account the latest economically feasible technical advances.

Several Directives have been adopted in order to lay down limit values for the emission of the substances mentioned in List I of the Annexe to Directive 76/464/EEC. These Directives cover the emission of mercury in the chlor-alkali electrolysis sector[1] and in other sectors[2], cadmium[3], hexachlorocyclohexane[4], carbon tetrachloride, DDT, pentachlorophenol[5], hexachlorobenzole, hexachlorobutanium, chloroform[6], 1,2-dichloroethane, trichloroethylene, perchloroethylene and trichlorobenzole[7].

Directive 86/280/EEC introduces a monitoring procedure, laid down in Article 6, paragraph 3 of Directive 76/464/EEC and consolidates the procedures and application rules to avoid repetition in every subsidiary Directive adopted in application of Directive 76/464/EEC and to speed up the work for all the priority substances mentioned in List I.

---

[1]   Council Directive 82/176/EEC, of 22 March 1982, on limit values and quality objectives for mercury discharges by the chlor-alkali electrolysis industry (OJ L 81, 27.03.1982, p. 29). See also Community Legislation concerning the environment, Volume 7, Water, first edition, p. 210 and xli.

[2]   Council Directive 84/156/EEC, of 8 March 1984, on limit values and quality objectives for mercury discharges by sectors other than the chlor-alkali electrolysis industry (OJ L 74, 17.03.1984, p. 49). See also Community Legislation concerning the environment, Volume 7, Water, first edition, p. 277 and xliv.

[3]   Council Directive 83/531/EEC, of 26 September 1983, on limit values and quality objectives for cadmium discharges (OJ L 291, 24.10.1983, p. 1). See also Community Legislation concerning the environment, Volume 7, Water, first edition, p. 253 and xlii.

[4]   Council Directive 84/491/EEC, of 9 October 1984, on limit values and quality objectives for discharges of hexachlorocyclohexane (OJ L 274, 17.10.1984, p. 11). See also Community Legislation concerning the environment, Volume 7, Water, first edition, p. 302 and xlv.

[5]   Council Directive 86/280/EEC, of 12 June 1986, on limit values and quality objectives for discharges of certain dangerous substances included in list I of the Annexe to Directive 76/464/EEC (OJ L 181, 04.07.1986, p. 16). See also Community Legislation concerning the environment, Volume 7, Water, first edition, p. 347 and xlvii.

[6]   Council Directive 88/347/EEC, of 16 June 1988, amending Annexe II to Directive 86/280/EEC, on limit values and quality objectives for discharges of certain dangerous substances included in list I of the Annexe to Directive 76/464/EEC (OJ L 158, 25.06.1988, p. 35). See also Community Legislation concerning the environment, Volume 7, Water, first edition, p. 449.

[7]   Council Directive 90/415/EEC, of 27 July 1990, amending Annexe II to Directive 86/280/EEC on limit values and quality objectives for discharges of certain dangerous substances included in list I of the Annexe to Directive 76/464/EEC (OJ L 219, 14.08.1990, p. 49). See also Community Legislation concerning the environment, Volume 7, Water, first edition, p. 452.

Directive 86/280/EEC also lays down the elaboration of specific programmes to avoid or eliminate pollution from the significant sources of the substances mentioned in List II of the Annexe to Directive 76/464/EEC (including multiple and diffuse sources) other than sources of waste subject to the Community limit values or national emission standards.

Discharge of dangerous substances in groundwater

Directive 80/68/EEC[1] aims at preventing the pollution of groundwater by the substances mentioned in Lists I and II of the Annexe and intends to reduce or eliminate the consequences of its present pollution.

The Member States ban the direct discharge into groundwater of all the substances appearing in List I. Concerning the indirect discharge of these substances in groundwater, the Member States will first investigate the possibilities of warehousing and eliminating these substances before they accept or reject these possibilities.

However, authorisation for direct and indirect emissions into groundwater of the substances appearing in List II is always preceded by an investigation. Among other things, this authorisation must include the maximum admissible quality of a substance which the emissions may contain. This authorisation is granted for a limited period and is re-examined every four years.

Council Resolution 95/C 59/02[2] invites the Commission to revise Directive 80/86/EEC by integrating the protection of groundwater in a general fresh water policy, including fresh water protection.

Treatment of urban waste water

Directive 91/271/EEC[3] concerns the prevention of environmental deterioration due to discharges of urban waste water and waste water produced by certain industrial sectors. For this reason, all built-up areas will be equipped with urban waste water collecting systems by 31 December 2000 or by 31 December

---

[1] Council Directive 80/68/EEC, of 17 December 1979, on the protection of groundwater against pollution caused by certain dangerous substances (OJ L 20, 26.01.1980, p. 43). See also Community Legislation concerning the environment, Volume 7, Water, first edition, p. 161 and xxxviii.

[2] Council Resolution 92/C 59/02, of 25 February 1992, on the future Community groundwater policy (OJ C 59, 06.03.1992, p. 2).

[3] Council Directive 91/271/EEC, of 21 May 1991, concerning urban waste water treatment (OJ L 135, 30.05.1991, p. 40). See also Community Legislation concerning the environment, Volume 7, Water, first edition, p. 398.

2005, depending on the size of the built-up area. Water entering the collecting systems must undergo a secondary treatment. This treatment generally involves a biological treatment with a secondary settlement or another process in which the requirements defined in table 1 on Annexe 1 are respected.

Certain circumstances allow water discharges to undergo a less stringent treatment provided that detailed studies ascertain that these discharges will not alter the state of the environment. This is the case for waste water emitted in high-altitude areas where an efficient biological treatment is seriously impaired due to low temperatures. A similar case is waste water emission from small built-up areas in regions less prone to environmental stress, provided that the waste water has at least undergone a primary treatment. However, a stricter treatment than the secondary treatment is imposed on waste water discharges from large built-up areas in more sensitive zones.

The Member States are required to define implementation programmes for this Directive by 31 December 1993. They must subsequently notify these programmes to the Commission by means of the presentation format set out in Decision 93/481/EEC[1].

Marine pollution

Telluric pollution

Council Decision 75/437/EEC[2] concerns the Community's approval of the Convention on the prevention of marine pollution from land-based sources (Paris Convention). Regarding this Convention, the Member States take all the appropriate measures to prevent marine pollution involving the direct or indirect introduction of substances or energy into the marine environment entailing hazards to human health, damage to living resources and to the marine environment, the impairment of maritime pleasure facilities or the prevention of the legitimate uses of the sea. In order to achieve this aim, the Member States ensure the urgent elimination of pollution resulting from the substances mentioned in part I of Annexe A to the present Convention. Moreover, they will reduce or even eliminate pollution resulting from the substances mentioned in part II of Annexe A. It is prohibited to discharge substances from

[1] Commission Decision 93/481/EEC, of 28 July 1993, concerning formats for the presentation of national programmes as laid down in Article 17 of Council Directive 91/271/EEC (OJ L 226, 07.09.1993, p. 23).

[2] Council Decision 75/437/EEC, of 3 March 1975, concluding the convention for the prevention of marine pollution from land-based sources (OJ L 194, 25.07.1975, p. 5). See also Community Legislation concerning the environment, Volume 7, Water, first edition, p. 8 and xxvii.

part II without obtaining a permit. Finally, pollution resulting from radioactive substances from part III of Annexe A must also be eliminated. The Member States must progressively implement a monitoring network to verify the existing pollution level and to verify the efficiency of the measures adopted within the framework of the Convention to reduce marine pollution from land-based sources.

Council Decision 85/613/EEC[1] concerns the approval of the measures and programmes relating to mercury and cadmium discharges within the framework of the Convention for the prevention of marine pollution.

Decision 87/57/EEC[2] approves the protocol extending the scope of activity of the Paris Convention to transatmospheric pollution of the sea.

Council Decision 83/101/EEC[3] concerns the Community's approval of the protocol relating to the protection of the Mediterranean against telluric pollution (Barcelona Convention). The Member States must take all necessary measures to prevent, diminish, combat and control the pollution of the Mediterranean due to emissions through river mouths, coastal industries and all other land-based sources of pollution on their territories. The Barcelona Convention also requires the Member States to design standards and schedules for the implementation of the measures and programmes aimed at eliminating these sources of pollution.

Pollution by hydrocarbons and other dangerous substances

Council Decision 81/420/EEC[4] concerns the Community's approval of the protocol relating to the co-operation in critical episodes of the fight against the pollution of the Mediterranean by hydrocarbons and other harmful substances. According to this protocol, the Member States adopt the necessary measures if

---

[1] Council Decision 85/613/EEC, of 20 December 1985, concerning the adoption, on behalf of the Community, of programmes and measures relating to mercury and cadmium discharges under the convention for the prevention of marine pollution from land-based sources (OJ L 375, 31.12.1985, p. 20). See also Community Legislation concerning the environment, Volume 7, Water, first edition, p. 313 and xlvi.

[2] Council Decision 87/57/EEC, of 22 December 1986, concluding the Protocol amending the Convention for the prevention of marine pollution from land-based sources (OJ L 24, 27.01.1987, p. 46).

[3] Council Decision 83/101/EEC, of 28 February 1983, concluding the Protocol for the protection of the Mediterranean Sea against pollution from land-based sources (OJ L 67, 12.03.1983, p. 1). See also Community Legislation concerning the environment, Volume 7, Water, first edition, p. 237 and xlii.

[4] Council Decision 81/420/EEC, of 19 May 1981, on the conclusion of the Protocol concerning co-operation in combating pollution of the Mediterranean Sea by oil and other harmful substances in cases of emergency (OJ L 162, 19.06.1981, p. 6). See also Community Legislation concerning the environment, Volume 7, Water, first edition, p. 201 and xli.

the massive presence, whether of accidental origin or resulting from a cumulative effect, of hydrocarbons or other dangerous substances polluting Mediterranean waters represents a serious and imminent threat to the marine environment, the coasts or the interests of one or several contracting parties to the protocol. The Member States must therefore implement a monitoring system of the Mediterranean and set up an information network in order to have all the necessary information on pollution caused by hydrocarbons and other harmful substances.

Decision 84/358/EEC[1] (Bonn Agreement) concerns the Community's approval of the co-operation in the fight against the pollution of the North Sea by hydrocarbons and other dangerous substances. The contracting parties ensure mutual co-operation in the case of an accident or when the quantity of hydrocarbons or other dangerous substances polluting the North Sea represents a serious and imminent threat to the coasts or the interests of one or several countries. The amendments to the Bonn Agreement have been approved on behalf of the Community by Decision 93/540/EEC[2].

Decision 86/85/EEC[3] institutes a system of information allowing the competent authorities of the Member States to access all the necessary data to monitor and to reduce pollution by a sizeable discharge of hydrocarbons and other harmful substances into the sea or into major inland waters.

Decision 93/550/EEC[4] approves on behalf of the Community the agreement relating to the co-operation for the protection of the coasts and waters of the north-east Atlantic Ocean. The contracting parties must ensure active mutual co-operation in order to prevent and to act promptly and efficiently in the case of an accident causing marine pollution by hydrocarbons or other dangerous substances.

---

[1] Council Decision 84/358/EEC, of 28 June 1984, concerning the conclusion of the Agreement for cooperation in dealing with pollution of the North Sea by oil and other harmful substances (OJ L 188, 16.07.1984, p. 7). See also Community Legislation concerning the environment, Volume 7, Water, first edition, p. 288 and xlv.

[2] Council Decision 93/540/EEC, of 18 October 1993, approving certain amendments to the Agreement for cooperation in dealing with pollution of the North Sea by oil and other harmful substances (Bonn Agreement) (OJ L 263, 22.10.1993, p. 51).

[3] Council Decision 86/85/EEC, of 6 March 1986, establishing a Community information system for the control and reduction of pollution caused by the spillage of hydrocarbons and other harmful substances at sea or in major inland waters (OJ L 77, 22.03.1986, p. 33). See also Community Legislation concerning the environment, Volume 7, Water, first edition, p. 335 and xlvii.

[4] Council Decision 93/550/EEC, of 20 October 1993, concerning the conclusion of the cooperation agreement for the protection of the coasts and waters of the north-east Atlantic against pollution(OJ L 267, 28.10.1993, p. 20).

Pollution by discharges from ships and aircraft

Council Decision 77/585/EEC[1] concerns the Community's approval of both the Convention on the Protection of the Mediterranean against pollution and the protocol relating to the prevention of pollution of the Mediterranean by discharges from ships and aircraft.

Under the Convention, the contracting countries take the necessary measures, whether individually or collectively, to prevent, reduce and combat pollution in the Mediterranean area and to protect and improve the marine environment in this area.

The protocol more particularly concerns the fight against pollution by discharges from ships and aircraft. It stipulates that the Member States must ban any discharge of waste and of the dangerous substances listed in Annexe I. Discharges of the waste mentioned in Annexe II require a specific licence obtained in advance. Moreover, it is generally assumed that the discharge of any other kind of waste and dangerous substances requires a general licence. The Member States instruct their ships and aircraft to monitor the sea as well as the authorised services to notify any discharge in contravention to this protocol, thus ensuring the correct implementation of the measures taken.

The Italian legislative ban only imposed on vessels flying the Italian flag on emitting harmful substances beyond Italian territorial waters should not imply a violation of the principle of non-discrimination by nationality of the maritime services. Indeed, in accordance with the stipulations of international public law, Italy may only exercise its authority beyond its territorial waters on ships flying the Italian flag. Consequently, Italy cannot complain that a Member State is apprehending only those vessels on which that State has the right to exercise its authority outside the territorial waters of its jurisdiction[2].

Pollution of the Baltic Sea

Decision 94/156/EEC[3] approves, on behalf of the Community, the 1974 Helsinki Convention on the protection of the marine environment in the Baltic

---

[1] Council Decision 77/585/EEC, of 25 July 1977, concluding the Convention for the protection of the Mediterranean Sea against pollution and the Protocol for the prevention of the pollution of the Mediterranean Sea by dumping from ships and aircraft (OJ L 240, 19.09.1977, p. 13). See also Community Legislation concerning the environment, Volume 7, Water, first edition, p. 59 and xxxii.

[2] Case C 379/92, Pretura di Ravenna vs. Peralta, 14.07.1994, Rec. 1994, I-34533

[3] Council Decision 94/156/EC, of 21 February 1994, on the accession of the Community to the Convention on the Protection of the Marine Environment of the Baltic Sea Area 1974 (Helsinki Convention) (OJ L 73, 16.03.1994, p. 19).

Sea Area. This Convention aims at preventing or reducing any form of pollution of the waters and the bed of the Baltic Sea by restricting or prohibiting the discharge of certain dangerous substances and certain types of waste. A commission for the protection of the marine environment of the Baltic Sea was set up to ensure the efficient implementation of the Convention. The Convention was revised in 1992[1]. The major amendments concern reinforced co-operation between the contracting parties to ensure the ecological restoration of the Baltic Sea and increasing information and public awareness with regard to the actions undertaken.

Pollution of rivers

Protection of the Rhine against pollution

Council Decision 77/586/EEC[2] approves, on behalf of the Community, the conclusion to the Convention on the protection of the Rhine against chemical pollution and the conclusion of the additional agreement on the international commission for the protection of the Rhine against pollution. Under the Convention, the Member States are required to take the necessary measures to eliminate the pollution of the surface waters of the Rhine by the particularly harmful substances listed in its Annexe I as well as to reduce the pollution of the Rhine by the substances mentioned in Annexe II. In order to achieve these aims, emissions of the substances from Annexe I require an authorisation obtained in advance. This authorisation must include limit values for the substances contained in these emissions. Moreover, emissions of the substances from Annexe II are included in a Regulation by the national authorities in order to severely restrict them.

---

[1] Council Decision 94/157/EC, of 21 February 1994, on the conclusion, on behalf of the Community, of the Convention on the Protection of the Marine Environment of the Baltic Sea Area (Helsinki Convention as revised in 1992) (OJ L 73, 16.03.1994, p. 1).

[2] Council Decision 77/586/EEC, of 25 July 1977, concluding the Convention for the protection of the Rhine against chemical pollution and an Additional Agreement to the Agreement, signed in Berne on 29 April 1963, concerning the International Commission for the Protection of the Rhine against Pollution (OJ L 240, 19.09.1977, p. 35). See also Community Legislation concerning the environment, Volume 7, Water, first edition, p. 87 and xxxiii.

Protection of the Elbe

Decision 91/598/EEC[1] approves, on behalf of the Community, of the Convention on the protection of the Elbe. The Convention institutes an international commission to prevent pollution of the Elbe. On 9 December 1991, an additional protocol to the Convention was adopted by the contracting parties to grant the commission the legal personality and the power to contract in order to accomplish the obligations imposed by the Convention. The protocol's approval on behalf of the Community is included in Decision 93/114/EEC[2].

Quality objectives for surface water

Five Directives on the quality objectives for water have been adopted: water for human consumption, bathing water, fresh water for fish and shellfish waters. In most cases, quality objectives imply on the one hand non-binding "guideline" values which Member States should try to achieve and on the other hand "mandatory" values imposed on the Member States by virtue of public health standards.

Surface waters for human consumption

In 1975, Directive 75/440/EEC[3] was adopted concerning the quality of surface waters for human consumption in the Member States. The Directive, which all Member States must apply to their national as well as to their border-crossing waters, divide surface waters into three groups of limit values. These limit values correspond to models of purification treatment procedures. The water groups correspond to three qualities of surface waters based on their physical, chemical and microbiological characteristics. Member States are required to take water samples regularly which must meet the mandatory quality objectives and should try to meet the guideline values from Annexe II of the present Directive. Surface waters are considered to be in conformity with the quality objectives when 95% of the samples taken comply with the values specified in

---

[1] Council Decision 91/598/EEC, of 18 November 1991, concerning the conclusion of the Convention on the International Commission for the Protection of the Elbe (OJ L 1991, 23.11.1991, p. 25).

[2] Council Decision 93/114/EEC, of 15 February 1993, concerning the conclusion of the Protocol to the Convention of 8 October 1990 between the Governments of the Federal Republic of Germany and of the Czech and Slovak Federal Republic and the European Economic Community on the International Commission for the Protection of the Elbe (OJ L 1991, 23.11.1991, p. 25).

[3] Council Directive 75/440/EEC of 16 June 1975, concerning the quality required of surface water intended for the abstraction of drinking water in the Member States (OJ L 194, 25.07.1975, p. 26). See also Community Legislation concerning the environment, Volume 7, Water, first edition, p. 27 and xxx.

Annexe II. However, it is always permissible for Member States to adopt more stringent values than those stipulated by this Directive.

Directive 79/869/EEC[1] concerns the methods of measurement and the frequency of sampling. This Directive was adopted by virtue of Article 5, paragraph 2 of Directive 75/440/EEC in order to harmonise sampling methods in the Community. This Directive concerns the methods of measurement and frequency of sampling and analysis of the parameters listed in Annexe II to Directive 75/440/EEC.

Directive 80/778/EEC[2], adopted in 1980, establishes the standards to be met by water for human consumption. This Directive stipulates the maximum quantities and guideline quantities of the different constituent elements of water. The analysis models and frequencies are stipulated in the Annexe to the Directive. The Member States are required to monitor the quality of water for human consumption. The frequency of monitoring, however, depends on the quality of the water.

Bathing water

Directive 76/160/EEC[3] stipulates the quality objectives for bathing water, including fresh water, running as well as stagnant, and sea water, excluding water for therapeutic uses and for swimming pools. The Directive establishes a minimum quality for bathing water on the basis of physicochemical and microbiological parameters. The Member States must ensure that their bathing water meets the limit values established in the Annexe to Directive 76/160/EEC within a maximum period of 10 years from its notification. However, exemptions regarding the States' obligation to have their waters meet the Directive's stipulations are set out in Articles 4, paragraphs 3 and 5, paragraphs 2 and 8.

---

[1] Council Directive 79/869/EEC of 9 October 1979, concerning the methods of measurement and frequencies of sampling and analysis of surface water intended for the abstraction of drinking water in the Member States (OJ L 271, 29.10.1979, p. 26). See also Community Legislation concerning the environment, Volume 7, Water, first edition, p. 150 and xxxix.

[2] Council Directive 80/778/EEC of 15 July 1980, relating to the quality of water intended for human consumption (OJ L 229, 30.08.1980, p. 11). See also Community Legislation concerning the environment, Volume 7, Water, first edition, p. 186 and xlii.

[3] Council Directive 76/160/EEC of 8 December 1975, concerning the quality of bathing water (OJ L 31, 05.02.1976, p. 1). See also Community Legislation concerning the environment, Volume 7, Water, first edition, p. 38 and xxxi.

In the case of the Commission vs. the United Kingdom[1], the Court of Justice stated that, apart from the exemptions explicitly stipulated, no specific circumstances can be invoked to justify non-compliance with Directive 76/160/EEC which imposes the achievement of certain results. Thus, adopting measures that are reasonably feasible is not enough by virtue of the obligation to achieve a result. This also justifies the conclusion that the United Kingdom did not comply with the obligations stipulated in Article 4 of the Directive.

Fresh water for fish

Directive 78/659/EEC[2] stipulates the quality objectives for fresh water and applies to the waters which the Member States consider to be in need of protection or improvement in order to be fit for fish. In order to achieve the aforementioned objectives, Member States establish programmes aimed at reducing pollution and ensuring that the waters considered meet the values shown in the Annexe to Directive 78/659/EEC within a maximum of five years.

Shellfish waters

Directive 79/923/EEC[3] defines the quality objectives for shellfish waters and applies to coastal and salt waters which the Member States consider to be in need of protection or improvement in order to allow shellfish to live in it and to contribute to the quality of the shellfish with a view to human consumption. In order to achieve this objective, the Member States establish programmes aimed at reducing pollution and ensuring that the waters considered meet the values shown in the Annexe to Directive 79/923/EEC within a maximum period of six years.

---

[1] Case C 56/90, Commission vs. United Kingdom, 14.07.1993, Rec. 1993, I-4109.

[2] Council Directive 78/659/EEC of 18 July 1978, on the quality of fresh waters needing protection or improvement in order to support fish life (OJ L 222, 14.08.1978, p. 1). See also Community Legislation concerning the environment, Volume 7, Water, first edition, p. 132 and xxxviii.

[3] Council Directive 79/923/EEC of 30 October 1979, on the quality required of shellfish water (OJ L 281, 10.11.1979, p. 47). See also Community Legislation concerning the environment, Volume 7, Water, first edition, p. 163 and xl.

Pollution by specific substances

Detergents

Directive 73/404/EEC[1] aims at approximating the Member States Legal Systems with a view to ensuring the biodegradability of detergents. The Directive applies to products of which the composition has specifically been designed to contribute to the development of detergency consisting of essential compounds (surfactants) and additional compounds. To achieve the objective set out in Directive 73/404/EEC, the Member States are required to prohibit the sale and the use of detergents whose average biodegradability regarding surfactants is less than 90% including the anionic, cationic and non-ionic categories and ampholytes. Moreover, normal use of these products must not be harmful to the health of humans and animals.

However, the Member States are authorised to allow certain exemptions, which are limited in time, for slightly foaming alkalioxides, which is an additive used in products for dishwashers, and for certain alkyl and alkylaryl-polyglycol ethers used in cleaning products for the food and metallurgical industries. Directive 86/94/EEC[2] sets 31 December 1989 as the deadline.

Directive 73/404/EEC concerns the adoption of Directives establishing monitoring methods in order to comply with the stipulations of the aforementioned Directive. Council Directive 73/405/EEC[3] established monitoring methods for anionic surfactants and Directive 82/242/EEC[4] for non-ionic surfactants.

---

[1] Council Directive 73/404/EEC of 22 November 1973, on the approximation of the laws of the Member States relating to detergents (OJ L 347, 17.12.1973, p. 1).
See also Community Legislation concerning the environment, Volume 7, Water, first edition, p. 2 and xxviii.

[2] Council Directive 86/94/EEC of 10 March 1986, amending for the second time Directive 73/404/EEC, on the approximation of the laws of the Member States relating to detergents (OJ L 80, 25.03.1986, p. 51). See also Community Legislation concerning the environment, Volume 7, Water, first edition, p. 436.

[3] Council directive 73/405/CEE of 10 November 1973, (OJ L 347, 17.12.1973, p. 53).

[4] Council Directive 82/242/EEC of 31 March 1982, on the approximation of the laws of the Member States relating to methods of testing the biodegradability of non-ionic surfactants and amending Directive 73/404/EEC (OJ L 109, 22.04.1982, p. 1). See also Community Legislation concerning the environment, Volume 7, Water, first edition, p. 236 and xlv.

Washing machines

Decision 93/430/EEC[1] stipulates the ecological criteria for the awarding of the Community Eco-label to washing machines.

Dishwashers

Decision 93/431/EEC[2] stipulates the ecological criteria for the award of the Community Eco-label to dishwashers.

Pollution by nitrates from agricultural sources

In 1991, the Council adopted a Directive[3] which aims to reduce pollution by nitrates from agricultural sources. This aim of the Directive is to prevent excessive concentrations of nitrates in the water by reducing the use of chemical fertilisers and the noxious effects of intensive production. These objectives will be achieved by limiting the use of manure to the absorption capacity of the fields. The Directive not only covers the storage and use of fertilisers containing nitrogen and effluents from animal husbandry, but also procedures for agricultural management and waste water treatment.

---

[1] Commission Decision 93/430/EEC, of 28 June 1993, establishing the ecological criteria for the awarding of the Community eco-label to washing machines (OJ L 198, 07.08.1993, p. 35).

[2] Commission Decision 93/431/EEC, of 28 June 1993, establishing the ecological criteria for the awarding of the Community eco-label to dishwashers (OJ L 198, 07.08.1993, p. 38).

[3] Council Directive 91/676/EEC, of 12 December 1991, concerning the protection of waters against pollution caused by nitrates from agricultural sources (OJ L 375, 31.12.1991, p. 1).

Summary of the Legislation

Council Decision 91/598/EEC[1] — Protection of the Elbe

This Decision approves, in the name of the Community, the convention on the international commission for the protection of the Elbe.

This convention implies the creation of an international commission to prevent the pollution of the Elbe and its hydrographic basin.

Council Directive 91/676/EEC[2] — Protection of waters against pollution caused by nitrates from agricultural sources

This Directive aims at reducing the pollution of waters by nitrates from agricultural sources as well as preventing any new pollution of this kind.

The Member States determine the waters affected by or susceptible to pollution. Areas on their territory known to feed the aforementioned waters and thus contributing to their pollution are defined as vulnerable areas. A List of vulnerable areas is notified to the Commission and is reviewed at least every four years.

In order to ensure a general level of protection against pollution for all waters, a code of good agricultural practice is voluntarily implemented by farmers. If necessary, the Member States will ensure the education and information of farmers in order to promote the implementation of the code of good agricultural practice.

Action programmes regarding the vulnerable areas are implemented with a maximum delay of four years upon their elaboration. They must contain measures aimed at preventing the spread of any fertiliser containing nitrogen and measures aimed at limiting the spread of effluent from animal husbandry. To this end, they must contain the measures adopted by the Member States regarding the code of good agricultural practice. It is allowed for additional

---

[1] Council Decision 91/598/EEC, of 18 November 1991, concerning the conclusion of the Convention on the International Commission for the Protection of the Elbe (OJ L 321, 23.11.1991, p. 24).

[2] Council Directive 91/676/EEC, of 12 December 1991, concerning the protection of waters against pollution caused by nitrates from agricultural sources (OJ L 375, 31.12.1991, p. 1).

measures to be adopted if the obligatory measures prove insufficient to achieve the objectives of the present Directive. These measures are opted for in accordance with their effectiveness and their cost in comparison with other possible preventive actions. Monitoring programmes are designed to evaluate the action programmes' efficiency.

In order to define and review the vulnerable areas, reference methods for the nitrogen level are elaborated.

A committee charged with assisting the Commission regarding the Directive's implementation and its adaptation to technical progress, has been instituted.

Every four years, the Member States submit a report to the Commission containing a report on the preventive actions, a map of polluted areas and areas susceptible to pollution, the action programmes and the results of monitoring their efficiency. The Commission publishes a summarised report based on this information which is transmitted to the European Parliament and to the Council. A Member States' report to the Council on the implementation of the present Directive is due on 1 January 1998.

Council Resolution 92/C 59/02[1] — The groundwater policy

This Resolution is a means by which the Council asks the Commission to propose an action programme regarding the protection of groundwater and to elaborate a proposal to review Directive 80/68/EEC[2] tackling the protection of groundwater against pollution caused by certain substances of a hazardous nature. This Directive must be included in a general fresh water policy including fresh water protection.

---

[1] Council Resolution 92/C 59/02, of 25 February 1992, on the future Community groundwater policy (OJ C 59, 06.03.1992, p. 2).

[2] Council Directive 80/68/EEC, of 17 December 1979, on the protection of groundwater against pollution caused by certain dangerous substances (OJ L 20, 26.01.1986, p. 43). See also Community environmental Legislation, Volume 7, Water, first edition, p. 161 and xxxviii.

Commission Decision 92/316/EEC[1] — Aid in favour of an environmentally-sound disposal of manure

.This Decision implies the Council's conviction that the aid, the Netherlands intend to award in favour of an environmentally-sound disposal of the excess of manure, is entirely in line with the common market. This aid is completely funded by taxing the aforementioned excess of manure. However, Its compatibility, being based upon Article 92, paragraph 3 of the EEC Treaty, goes as far as the aid's cost does not exceed the fixed cost of the SLM (Stichtelijke Landelijke Mestbank). The aid to finance the variable cost can only be considered compatible in the initial period, ending on 31 December 1994, after which period the aid may no longer be awarded.

A report on the activities of the SLM and their funding will annually be submitted to the Commission. The Netherlands will inform the Commission about the measures taken to comply with the Decision.

Commission Decision 92/446/EEC[2] — Questionnaires relating to Directives in the water sector

This Decision adopts outlines of questionnaires relating to Directives stipulating limit values for emissions of certain hazardous substances in waters or defining their quality objectives.

Council Decision 93/114/EEC[3] — Protection of the Elbe

This Decision approves, on behalf of the Community, the protocol to the Convention of 8 October 1990 between the governments of the Federal Republic of Germany, the Czech and Slovak Federal Republic and the European Economic Community, on the international commission for the protection of the Elbe.

This protocol grants the commission the legal personality and the power to contract according to German law in order to accomplish the obligations imposed by the convention.

---

[1] Commission Decision 92/316/EEC, of 11 March 1992, concerning aid envisaged by the Netherlands Government in favour of an environmentally-sound disposal of manure (of which the Dutch text is the sole proof) (OJ L 170, 25.06.1992, p. 34).

[2] Commission Decision 92/446/EEC, of 27 July 1992, concerning questionnaires relating to directives in the water sector (OJ 247, 27.08.1992, p. 10).

[3] Council Decision 93/114/EEC, of 15 February 1993, concerning the conclusion of the Protocol to the Convention of 8 October 1990 between the Governments of the Federal Republic of Germany and of the Czech and Slovak Federal Republic and the European Economic Community on the International Commission for the Protection of the Elbe (OJ L 45, 23.02.1993, p. 25).

Council Regulation (EEC) No 1541/93[1] — Ground frost

This Regulation authorises, for the campaigns of 1994/1995 and 1995/1996, a non-rotational set-aside rate for ground frost which is five percent higher than the rotational rate. An increase of this rate by three percent is only authorised in vulnerable areas as established in Directive 91/676/EEC (see above) provided there is a significant decrease of the use of fertiliser.

This policy allows an improved production control. The Commission will draw up a report regarding the 1995/1996-campaign accompanied by proposals if need be.

Commission Decision 93/430/EEC[2] — The Community eco-label for washing machines

This Decision applies to washing machines with a frontal or vertical loading device sold to the public excluding twin-tub washing machines for washing and draining, and washing / drying machines. A washing machine's ecological performance essentially depends on its energy consumption as well as on its water and detergent consumption based upon the most significant impact of these machines on the environment; optimum utilisation criteria for washing machines allowing to diminish their impact on the environment and perform-ance criteria for washing and rinsing.

The definition of the type of washing machines in the present Decision and the specific ecological criteria for this type of machines are only valid until 30 June 1996.

---

[1] Council Regulation (EEC) No 1541/93, of 14 June 1993, fixing the non-rotational set-aside rate referred to in Article 7 of Regulation (EEC) No 1765/92 (OJ L 154, 25.06.1993, p. 1).

[2] Commission Decision 93/430/EEC, of 28 June 1993, establishing the ecological criteria for the award of the Community eco-label to washing machines (OJ L 198, 07.08.1993, p. 35).

Commission Decision 93/431/EEC[1] — The Community eco-label for dishwashers

This Decision applies to dishwashers sold to the public. Their ecological performance depends on the essential ecological criteria for energy and water consumption based upon the most significant impact of these machines on the environment; optimum utilisation criteria for dishwashers allowing to diminish their impact on the environment and performance criteria for washing and drying.

The definition of the type of dishwashers in the present Decision and the specific ecological criteria for this type of machines are only valid until 30 June 1996.

Commission Regulation (EEC) No 2158/93[2] — Safety of human life at sea and prevention of pollution from ships

Concerning the ships' transfer between the register books of Member States, the 1974 SOLAS Convention and the MARPOL Convention of 1973/1978 are limited, within the Community, to the rules operative upon the adoption of the Regulation (EEC) 613/91[3] on 4 March 1991. This Regulation deals with the shift of register books for ships in the Community. The 1974 SOLAS has been amended several times between 1988 and 1990 in order to improve the security of ships. The MARPOL Convention of 1973/1978 was amended on 4 July 1991 to reinforce the standards of prevention of pollution from ships. These amendments took effect on an international scale on 1 February 1992 and 4 April 1993 respectively.

The present Regulation stipulates the amendments to these conventions to come into force in aid of Regulation (EEC) 613/91, in order to ensure the application of the reinforced standards for maritime security and the prevention of pollution in the Community.

---

[1]   Commission Decision 93/431/EEC, of 28 June 1993, establishing the ecological criteria for the award of the Community eco-label to dishwashers (OJ L 198, 07.08.1993, p. 38).

[2]   Commission Regulation No 2158/93, of 28 July 1993, concerning the application of amendments to the International Convention for the Safety of Life at Sea, 1974, and to the International Convention for the Prevention of Pollution from ships, 1973, for the purpose of Council Regulation (EEC) No 613/91 (OJ L 194, 03.08.1993, p. 5).

[3]   Council Regulation 613/91, of 4 March 1991, regarding the transfer of ships between register books within the Community (OJ L 68, 15.03.1991, p. 1).

Commission Decision 93/481/EEC[1] — Treatment of urban waste water

This Decision applies Article 17, paragraph 4 of the Directive 91/271/EEC[2] by elaborating formats for presentations to be adopted by the Member States for their reports to the Commission. These reports contain the Member State's national programme for the implementation of Directive 91/271/EEC.

Commission Directive 93/80/EEC[3] — Transitional measures for Germany

This Directive authorises the prolongation until 31 December 1995 of the implementation delays of certain Community Regulations regarding the disposal of hazardous substances in the former Democratic Republic of Germany as established in Directive 90/656/EEC[4].

The environmental problems in the former Democratic Republic of Germany are considerably bigger than the estimations on which the implementation date, 31 December 1992, of the Community Regulations was based. These problems are certainly due to the obsolete production units located in the Democratic Republic of Germany emitting hazardous substances in surface waters. Directive 93/80/EEC subsequently extends the implementation date till 31 December 1995, taking into account the time required to adapt the aforementioned production units in order to meet the stipulations of the Directives mentioned in Article 3 of Directive 90/656/EEC.

---

[1] Commission Decision 93/481/EEC, of 28 July 1993, concerning formats for the presentation of national programmes as foreseen by Article 17 of Council Directive 91/271/EEC (OJ L 226, 07.09.1993, p. 23).

[2] Council Directive 91/271/EEC, of 21 May 1991, concerning the treatment of urban waste water (OJ L 135, 30.05.1991, p. 40).

[3] Commission Directive 93/80/EEC, of 23 September 1993, amending Council Directive 90/656/EEC on the transitional measures applicable in Germany with regard to certain Community provisions relating to the protection of the environment (OJ L 256, 14.10.1993, p. 32).

[4] Council Directive 90/656/EEC, of 4 December 1990, regarding the transitional measures for Germany with respect to certain Community provisions for environmental protection (OJ L 353, 17.12.1990, p. 59).

Council Decision 93/540/EEC[1] — the North Sea

This Decision implies the Community's approbation of the amendments, adopted by every participant on their first meeting, to the agreement regarding the co-operation in the fight against the pollution of the North Sea by hydrocarbons and hazardous substances (Bonn Agreement).

The amendments not only broaden the agreement's scope to monitoring in order to detect pollution and to prevent violations of the Regulations aimed at preventing pollution, but also adjust the geographic border of the south of the Skaggerak as stipulated in Article 2 of the agreement.

Council Decision 93/550/EEC[2] — The protection of the coasts and waters of the north-east Atlantic against pollution.

This Decision implies the Community's approbation of the agreement on co-operation to protect the coasts and the waters of the north-east Atlantic against pollution.

The parties agree to take all the necessary measures to prepare themselves to tackle pollution caused by hydrocarbons or other substances of a hazardous nature. These measures imply a minimum equipment and maintenance as well as an action plan to deal with an oil spill and other dangerous substances. It also implies a preventive system as well as an outline to fight marine pollution and a framing of personnel training in order to improve the wakefulness of the organisations against pollution.

A system of information and active co-operation is established between the participant parties in order to enable a prompt and efficient action in case of marine pollution.

The north-east Atlantic is divided into areas. Each participant party is required to estimate the pollution occurring in his area and to inform, if need be, the other participants. Areas of co-decision may well be stipulated. In this case, the party responsible for a zone affected by pollution, not only informs the neighbouring participants but also asks them to make an estimation of the pollution's seriousness and, if necessary, to draw up a common plan of action.

---

[1]   Council Decision 93/540/EEC, of 18 October 1993, approving certain amendments to the Agreement for cooperation in dealing with pollution of the North Sea by oil and other harmful substances (Bonn Agreement) (OJ L 263, 22.10.1993, p. 51).

[2]   Council Decision 93/550/EEC, of 20 October 1993, concerning the conclusion of the cooperation agreement for the protection of the coasts and waters of the north east Atlantic against pollution (OJ L 267, 28.10.1993, p. 20).

The participant parties introduce means of monitoring navigation by maritime traffic services.

In the absence of bilateral or multilateral agreements with respect to funding provisions, each participant is required to finance the cost of his own actions in the fight against marine pollution.

Council and Commission Decision 94/1/ECSC, EC[1] — The European Economic Area

The participant parties agree to preserve, protect and improve the quality of the environment and to contribute to the protection of human health and to ensure a rational and economical use of natural resources. In this respect a whole range of Community Directives concerning the environment apply to the entire European Economic Area. These measures of protection, however, do not obstruct the participants to maintain or stipulate reinforced measures of protection in line with the present agreement.

Their efforts with respect to the environment are based on the principles of preventive action, tackling environmental problems, preferably at source, and the principle of "the polluter pays". The stipulations concerning the environment must be inserted in the other policies of the participant parties.

Council Decision 94/156/EC[2] — The Baltic Sea

This Decision stipulates the Community's participation in the Convention on the protection of the marine environment of the Baltic Sea Area (Helsinki convention 1974).

The 1974 Helsinki Convention applies to the protection of the Baltic Sea marine environment, including the water, the depths of the Baltic Sea, together with the living resources and all other marine life it holds.

It is strictly forbidden to emit DDT and its derivatives as well as PCB and PCT into the Baltic Sea, either by air, or by waterways or in any other possible way.

---

[1] Decision 94/1/EC, ECSC of the Council and the Commission of 13 December 1993, on the conclusion of the agreement on the European Economic Area between the European Communities, their Member States and the Republic of Austria, the Republic of Finland, the Republic of Iceland, the Principality of Liechtenstein, the Kingdom of Norway, the Kingdom of Sweden and the Swiss Confederation (OJ L 1, 03.01.1994, p. 1).

[2] Council Decision 94/156/EC, of 21 February 1994, on the accession of the Community to the Convention on the Protection of the Marine Environment of the Baltic Sea Area 1974 (Helsinki Convention) (OJ L 73, 16.03.1994, p. 1).

Telluric pollution of the marine environment is reduced to a strict minimum. Pollution by hazardous substances and products mentioned in Annexe II is significantly restricted. The emission of large quantities of these substances requires a special permit issued beforehand by the competent national authority. However, in their fight against telluric pollution, the participant parties tend to achieve the presupposed objectives and tend to apply the criteria mentioned in Annexe III.

The participants also ensure the prevention of pollution by deliberate oil spills or other harmful substances, out of negligence or by accident as well as pollution by the emission of waste water and waste from ships. The problems for the Baltic Sea marine environment resulting from pleasure cruises, however, are softened.

Dumping waste in the Baltic Sea is strictly forbidden, except for dredgings of which the dumping still requires a permit, issued beforehand. Moreover, dumping is only sustained if it is considered the only way to lift the menace to human and marine life.

An active co-operation between the participant parties to the Convention is favoured in order to eliminate or to reduce to a strict minimum the pollution of the Baltic Sea by hydrocarbons and other hazardous substances.

A commission for the protection of the Baltic Sea marine environment has been instituted to ensure an efficient implementation of the Convention.

Council Decision 94/157/EC[1] — The Baltic Sea

This Decision approves, on behalf of the Community, the Convention regarding the protection of the Baltic Sea Marine environment (Helsinki Convention as revised in 1992).

The major change introduced by the 1992 revision of the Helsinki Convention, is the establishment of a framework of regional co-operation in order to ensure the ecological restoration of the Baltic Sea in view of the autoregeneration of the marine environment and the preservation of its ecological balance. The existing system of information is reinforced: every participant notifies the Commission about the measures adopted in favour of the Convention's implementation, the efficiency of these measures, the problems encountered and any kind of information regarding permits issued and data about the quality of the

---

[1] Council Decision 94/157/EC, of 21 February 1994, on the conclusion, on behalf of the Community, of the Convention on the Protection of the Marine Environment of the Baltic Sea Area (Helsinki Convention as revised in 1992) (OJ L 73, 16.03.1994, p. 19).

environment. The public accessing this information is highly favoured without, however, violating the rights of intellectual property including commercial and industrial confidentiality and without endangering national security or the confidential nature of personal data.

Council Resolution 94/C 135/02[1] — The integrated management of the coastal areas

The Council invites the Commission to propose a Community strategy for an integrated management of all coastal areas of the Community before November 1994. A move which fits in the fifth Community programme on environmental policy and action and on the creation of a long-term development. The aforementioned strategy will take into account the problems as well as the specific potentials of every zone, thus providing a framework for its preservation and long-term use.

---

[1] Council Resolution 94/C 135/02, of 6 May 1994, on a Community strategy, for integrated coastal-zone management (OJ C 135, 18.05.1994, p. 3).

Legislation concerning Water

COUNCIL DECISION 91/598/EEC[1]
of 18 November 1991
concerning the conclusion of the Convention on the International Commission for the Protection of the Elbe

THE COUNCIL OF THE EUROPEAN COMMUNITIES,

Having regard to the Treaty establishing the European Economic Community, and in particular Article 130s thereof,

Having regard to the proposal from the Commission[2],

Having regard to the opinion of the European Parliament[3],

Having regard to the opinion of the Economic and Social Committee[4],

Having regard to the Resolution of the Council and of the Representatives of the Governments of the Member States meeting within the Council of 19 October 1987 on the continuation and implementation of a European Community policy and action programme on the environment (1987-1992)[5], and the fourth action programme of the European Communities on the environment, annexed to the said Resolution, hereafter called 'Fourth Action Programme',

Whereas the Fourth Action Programme, in continuation of the earlier Action Programmes, lists amongst its main areas of activity, monitoring and control with a view to improving water quality and reducing pollution;

Whereas the Fourth Action Programme calls for active participation by the Community and its Member States in international action for the protection of the environment and attaches, in this framework, particular importance to bilateral liaisons with third countries;

Whereas the Convention on the International Commission for the Protection of the Elbe, signed in Magdeburg on 8 October 1990, provides in particular for the establishment of an international commission to prevent the pollution of the Elbe and its drainage area, as far as covered by this Convention;

---

[1]   OJ No L 321, 23. 11. 1991, p. 24.
[2]   OJ No C 93, 11. 4. 1991, p. 10.
[3]   OJ No C 158, 17. 6. 1991, p. 291.
[4]   OJ No C 191, 22. 7. 1991, p. 21.
[5]   OJ No C 328, 7. 12. 1987, p. 1.

Whereas the existing Community legislation on water pollution currently applies to the Elbe and its tributaries where they run through the territory of the Federal Republic of Germany;

Whereas it appears necessary for the Community to approve the Convention in order to attain one of the objectives of the Community as regards the preservation, protection and improvement of the quality of the environment, as provided for in the Single European Act;

Whereas the said Convention was signed on behalf of the Community on 8 October 1990,

HAS DECIDED AS FOLLOWS:

Article 1

The Convention on the International Commission for the Protection of the Elbe is hereby approved on behalf of the European Economic Community.

The text of the Convention is attached hereto.

Article 2

The President of the Council will, on behalf of the European Economic Community, inform the Federal Republic of Germany, in its capacity as depositary State, that the preconditions for the entry into force of the Convention have been fulfilled as far as the Community is concerned, in accordance with the first subparagraph of Article 18 of the Convention.

Done at Brussels, 18 November 1991.

For the Council

The President

J. E. ANDRIESSEN

CONVENTION
on the International Commission for the Protection of the Elbe
(EEC translation)

THE GOVERNMENTS OF THE FEDERAL REPUBLIC OF GERMANY AND OF THE CZECH AND SLOVAK FEDERAL REPUBLIC AND THE EUROPEAN ECONOMIC COMMUNITY
(hereinafter referred to as the 'contracting parties'),

CONCERNED about keeping the river Elbe free from pollution,

RESOLVED to prevent its further pollution and to improve its current state,

RECOGNIZING the need to make a sustained contribution to the reduction of pollution in the North Sea arising from the Elbe,

CONVINCED of the urgency of these tasks, and

INTENDING to increase the cooperation that already exists between the contracting parties in this area,

HAVE AGREED THE FOLLOWING:

Article 1

1.   The contracting parties shall cooperate in the International Commission for the Protection of the Elbe, hereinafter referred to as the Commission, to prevent the pollution of the Elbe and its drainage area.

2.   They shall in so doing in particular endeavour:

a) to enable use to be made of the river, in particular the obtaining of supplies of drinking water from bank-filtered waters and the agricultural use of the waters and sediments;

b) to achieve as natural an ecosystem as possible with a healthy diversity of species;

c) to reduce substantially the pollution of the North Sea from the Elbe area.

3.   In order to attain these objectives step-by-step, the contracting parties within the framework of the Commission shall determine the tasks to be carried

4

out as a priority in the form of work programmes with timetables. These programmes shall provide, inter alia, proposals for the application of state-of-the-art techniques for the reduction of emissions and for measures to reduce pollution from various sources.

4.   This Convention does not cover matters relating to the fishing industry and shipping; however, this does not exclude the consideration of matters relating to the protection of the waters against pollution caused by these activities.

Article 2

1.   In particular, the Commission shall:

a) prepare surveys showing major point sources of discharges of harmful materials (discharge charts), estimate water pollution from diffuse sources and extrapolate both of these,

b) propose limit values for the discharge of effluent,

c) propose specific quality objectives taking account of the requirements with regard to the use of the waters, the particular conditions for the protection of the North Sea and the natural aquatic communities,

d) propose and coordinate the implementation of joint programmes of measurements and investigations to demonstrate the quality of the waters, sediments and effluent and to describe the aquatic and coastal communities, and shall record and evaluate the findings,

e) compile standardized methods for the classification of water quality in the Elbe,

f) propose specific action for the reduction of discharges of harmful materials from the point sources of both local authorities and industry and from diffuse sources and further measures including timetables and a cost assessment,

g) propose protective measures to prevent water pollution resulting from accidents,

h) propose a uniform warning and alert system for the drainage area, to be updated according to experience,

i) describe the hydrological situation in the Elbe area and record the main influencing factors (Elbe monograph),

j) provide documentary evidence regarding the ecological importance of the various biotope elements of the waters and proposals regarding the improvement of conditions for aquatic and coastal communities,

k) discuss planned and, upon request by a delegation, existing types of utilization of the waters which may have serious international repercussions, including hydraulic structures and regulation of the waters,

l) promote cooperation in particular on scientific research projects and regarding the exchange of information especially on the state of technology,

m) prepare the basis for any regulation between the contracting parties regarding the protection of the Elbe and its drainage area.

2. The Commission shall furthermore be responsible for all other matters assigned to it by the contracting parties by joint agreement.

Article 3

This Convention shall apply in the territories in which the Treaty establishing the European Economic Community is applicable and under the terms of that Treaty, on the one hand, and in the territory of the Czech and Slovak Federal Republic, on the other hand.

Article 4

The contracting parties shall inform the Commission of all the basic matters required for the Commission to fulfil its tasks and of the measures taken and the total resources used therefor. The Commission may submit proposals to the contracting parties regarding improvements.

Article 5

1. The Commission shall consist of the delegations of the contracting parties. Each contracting party shall appoint a maximum of five delegates and their deputies, including the head of the delegation and his deputy.

2. Each delegation may call in experts which it appoints for the consideration of certain matters.

Article 6

1. The chairmanship of the Commission shall be held by the delegations of the contracting parties in turn. Details regarding the provision of a chairman shall be determined by the Commission and included in its rules of procedure; the delegation chairing the Commission shall appoint one of its members as

Chairman. This delegation may appoint a further delegate for the duration of its chairmanship.

2.   The Chairman shall, as a rule, not speak on behalf of his delegation during the meetings of the Commission.

Article 7

1.   The Commission shall meet at least once a year, when invited by the Chairman for a regular meeting at a place to be specified by him.

2.   Extraordinary meetings shall be convened by the Chairman if so requested by a delegation.

3.   The leaders of the delegations may confer between meetings of the Commission.

4.   The Chairman shall propose the agenda. Each delegation shall be entitled to include those items in the agenda which it wishes to have discussed. The order shall be decided by majority decision of the Commission.

Article 8

1.   Each delegation shall have one vote.

2.   Negotiations and decisions within the framework of this Convention as well as its implementation shall be conducted by the European Economic Community and the Federal Republic of Germany within their respective fields of competence. The European Economic Community shall not exercise its right to vote in cases in which the Federal Republic of Germany is competent and vice versa.

3.   The Commission's decisions and proposals shall, unless otherwise specified in this Convention, be unanimously adopted; a written procedure may take place in line with the conditions to be specified in the rules of procedure.

4.   Decisions nem. con. shall be deemed to be unanimous, provided all delegations are present.

Article 9

1.   The Commission shall set up working parties to carry out certain tasks.

2.   The working parties shall consist of the delegates or experts appointed by each delegation.

3.   The Commission shall determine the task and the number of members of each working party and shall appoint the Chairmen of such working parties.

Article 10

The Commission shall establish a secretariat for the preparation, implementation and support of its work. The headquarters of the secretariat shall be at Magdeburg. Further details shall be governed by the rules of procedure.

Article 11

The Commission may call on the services of especially suitable persons or establishments for the examination of special matters.

Article 12

The Commission shall adopt decisions regarding cooperation with other national and international organizations concerned with pollution control.

Article 13

The Commission shall provide the contracting parties with an activity report at least every two years and, as required, with further reports setting out in particular the results of investigations and their assessments.

Article 14

1.   Each contracting party shall bear the cost of its representation in the Commission and the working parties and the cost of the current investigations carried out in its territory.

2.   All other expenditure arising from the work of the Commission, including the costs of the secretariat, shall be divided among the contracting parties as follows:

Federal Republic of Germany		65,0%
Communauté économique européenne		2,5%
Czech and Slovak Federal Republic		32,5%
	Total :	100%

The Commission may also specify a different breakdown in certain cases.

Article 15

The Commission shall adopt rules of procedure.

Article 16

1.   Existing agreements and treaties shall remain unaffected.

2.   The Commission shall examine as soon as possible to what extent it is expedient to amend, supplement or annul agreements and treaties as referred to in paragraph 1 because of their contents or for other reasons; it shall draw up recommendations in respect of their amendment or annulment and of the conclusion of new agreements or treaties.

Article 17

The working languages of the Commission shall be German and Czech.

Article 18

This Convention shall enter into force on the day on which all signatories inform the Federal Republic of Germany as depositary that any preconditions for the entry into force required by the national laws have been fulfilled.

The Convention shall be concluded for an unlimited period. It may be denounced with five years' notice. The notice of denunciation is to be made in writing to the depositary, who will inform the other contracting parties. The notice of denunciation will take effect as of the day on which it is received by the depositary.

Article 19

This Convention, which is drawn up in original copies in the German and Czech languages, each text being equally binding, shall be deposited in the archives of the Government of the Federal Republic of Germany; the latter shall send a certified copy to each of the contracting parties.

Done at Magdeburg,

on the eighth day of October one thousand nine hundred and ninety

For the Government of the Federal Republic of Germany

For the European Economic Community

For the Government of the Czech and Slovak Federal Republic

COUNCIL DIRECTIVE 91/676/EEC[1]
of 12 December 1991
concerning the protection of waters against pollution caused by nitrates from agricultural sources

THE COUNCIL OF THE EUROPEAN COMMUNITIES,

Having regard to the Treaty establishing the European Economic Community, and in particular Article 130s thereof,

Having regard to the proposal from the Commission[2],

Having regard to the opinion of the European Parliament[3],

Having regard to the opinion of the Economic and Social Committee[4],

Whereas the nitrate content of water in some areas of Member States is increasing and is already high as compared with standards laid down in Council Directive 75/440/EEC of 16 June 1975 concerning the quality required of surface water intended for the abstraction of drinking water in the Member States[5], as amended by Directive 79/869/EEC[6], and Council Directive 80/778/EEC of 15 July 1980 relating to the quality of water intended for human consumption[7], as amended by the 1985 Act of Accession;

Whereas the fourth programme of action of the European Economic Communities on the environment[8] indicated that the Commission intended to make a proposal for a Directive on the control and reduction of water pollution resulting from the spreading or discharge of livestock effluents and the excessive use of fertilizers;

Whereas the reform of the common agricultural policy set out in the Commission's green paper 'Perspectives for the common agricultural policy' indicated that, while the use of nitrogen‾containing fertilizers and manures is necessary for Community agriculture, excessive use of fertilizers constitutes an environmental risk, that common action is needed to control the problem arising from

---

[1] OJ No L 375, 31. 12. 1991, p. 1.
[2] OJ No C 54, 3. 3. 1989, p. 4 and OJ No C 51, 2. 3. 1990, p. 12.
[3] OJ No C 158, 26. 6. 1989, p. 487.
[4] OJ No C 159, 26. 6. 1989, p. 1.
[5] OJ No L 194, 25. 7. 1975, p. 26.
[6] OJ No L 271, 29. 10. 1979, p. 44.
[7] OJ No L 229, 30. 8. 1980, p. 11.
[8] OJ No C 328, 7. 12. 1987, p. 1.

intensive livestock production and that agricultural policy must take greater account of environmental policy;

Whereas the Council resolution of 28 June 1988 of the protection of the North Sea and of other waters in the Community[1] invites the Commission to submit proposals for measures at Community level;

Whereas the main cause of pollution from diffuse sources affecting the Community's waters in nitrates from agricultural sources;

Whereas it is therefore necessary, in order to protect human health and living resources and aquatic ecosystems and to safeguard other legitimate uses of water, to reduce water pollution caused or induced by nitrates from agricultural sources and to prevent further such pollution; whereas for this purpose it is important to take measures concerning the storage and the application on land of all nitrogen compounds and concerning certain land management practices;

Whereas since pollution of water due to nitrates on one Member State can influence waters in other Member States, action at Community level in accordance with Article 130r is therefore necessary;

Whereas, by encouraging good agricultural practices, Member States can provide all waters with a general level of protection against pollution in the future;

Whereas certain zones, draining into waters vulnerable to pollution from nitrogen compounds, require special protection;

Whereas it is necessary for Member States to identify vulnerable zones and to establish and implement action programmes in order to reduce water pollution from nitrogen compounds in vulnerable zones;

Whereas such action programmes should include measures to limit the land-application of all nitrogen-containing fertilizers and in particular to set specific limits for the application of livestock manure;

Whereas it is necessary to monitor waters and to apply reference methods of measurement for nitrogen compounds to ensure that measures are effective;

Whereas it is recognized that the hydrogeology in certain Member States is such that it may be many years before protection measures lead to improvements in water quality;

---

[1] OJ No C 209, 9. 8. 1988, p. 3.

Whereas a Committee should be established to assist the Commission on matters relating to the implementation of this Directive and to its adaptation to scientific and technical progress;

Whereas Member States should establish and present to the Commission reports on the implementation of this Directive;

Whereas the Commission should report regularly on the implementation of this Directive by the Member States,

HAS ADOPTED THIS DIRECTIVE:

Article 1

This Directive has the objective of:

— reducing water pollution caused or induced by nitrates from agricultural sources and

— preventing further such pollution.

Article 2

For the purpose of this Directive:

a) 'groundwater': means all water which is below the surface of the ground in the saturation zone and in direct contact with the ground or subsoil;

b) 'freshwater': means naturally occurring water having a low concentration of salts, which is often acceptable as suitable for abstraction and treatment to produce drinking water;

c) 'nitrogen compound': means any nitrogen-containing substance except for gaseous molecular nitrogen;

d) 'livestock': means all animals kept for use or profit;

e) 'fertilizer': means any substance containing a nitrogen compound or nitrogen compounds utilized on land to enhance growth of vegetation; it may include livestock manure, the residues from fish farms and sewage sludge;

f) 'chemical fertilizer': means any fertilizer which is manufactured by an industrial process;

g)   'livestock manure': means waste products excreted by livestock or a mixture of litter and waste products excreted by livestock, even in processed form;

h)   'land application': means the addition of materials to land whether by spreading on the surface of the land, injection into the land, placing below the surface of the land or mixing with the surface layers of the land;

i)   'eutrophication': means the enrichment of water by nitrogen compounds, causing an accelerated growth of algae and higher forms of plant life to produce an undesirable disturbance to the balance of organisms present in the water and to the quality of the water concerned;

j)   'pollution': means the discharge, directly or indirectly, of nitrogen compounds from agricultural sources into the aquatic environment, the results of which are such as to cause hazards to human health, harm to living resources and to aquatic ecosystems, damage to amenities or interference with other legitimate uses of water;

k)   'vulnerable zone': means an area of land designated according to Article 3 (2).

Article 3

1.   Waters affected by pollution and waters which could be affected by pollution if action pursuant Article 5 is not taken shall be identified by the Member States in accordance with the criteria set out in Annex I.

2.   Member States shall, within a two⁻year period following the notification of this Directive, designate as vulnerable zones all known areas of land in their territories which drain into the waters identified according to paragraph 1 and which contribute to pollution. They shall notify the Commission of this initial designation within six months.

3.   When any waters identified by a Member State in accordance with paragraph 1 are affected by pollution from waters from another Member State draining directly or indirectly in to them, the Member States whose waters are affected may notify the other Member States and the Commission of the relevant facts.

The Member States concerned shall organize, where appropriate with the Commission, the concertation necessary to identify the sources in question and the measures to be taken to protect the waters that are affected in order to ensure conformity with this Directive.

4.   Member States shall review if necessary revise or add to the designation of vulnerable zones as appropriate, and at last every four years, to take into account changes and factors unforeseen at the time of the previous designation. They shall notify the Commission of any revision or addition to the designations within six months.

5.   Member States shall be exempt from the obligation to identify specific vulnerable zones, if they establish and apply action programmes referred to in Article 5 in accordance with this Directive throughout their national territory.

Article 4

1.   With the aim of providing for all waters a general level of protection against pollution, Member States shall, within a two⁻year period following the notification of this Directive:

 a) establish a code or codes of good agricultural practice, to be implemented by farmers on a voluntary basis, which should contain provisions covering at least the items mentioned in Annex II A;

 b) set up where necessary a programme, including the provision of training and information for farmers, promoting the application of the code(s) of good agricultural practice.

2.   Member States shall submit to the Commission details of their codes of good agricultural practice and the Commission shall include information on these codes in the report referred to in Article 11. In the light of the information received, the Commission may, if it considers it necessary, make appropriate proposals to the Council.

Article 5

1.   Within a two⁻year period following the initial designation referred to in Article 3 (2) or within one year of each additional designation referred to in Article 3 (4), Member States shall, for the purpose of realizing the objectives specified in Article 1, establish action programmes in respect of designated vulnerable zones.

2.   An action programme may relate to all vulnerable zones in the territory of a Member State or, where the Member State considers it appropriate, different programmes may be established for different vulnerable zones or parts of zones.

3.   Action programmes shall take into account:

a) available scientific and technical data, mainly with reference to respective nitrogen contributions originating from agricultural and other sources;

b) environmental conditions in the relevant regions of the Member State concerned.

4.   Action programmes shall be implemented within four years of their establishment and shall consist of the following mandatory measures:

a) the measures in Annex III;

b) those measures which Member States have prescribed in the code(s) of good agricultural practice established in accordance with Article 4, except those which have been superseded by the measures in Annex III.

5.   Member States shall moreover take, in the framework of the action programmes, such additional measures or reinforced actions as they consider necessary if, at the outset or in the light of experience gained in implementing the action programmes, it becomes apparent that the measures referred to in paragraph 4 will not be sufficient for achieving the objectives specified in Article 1. In selecting these measures or actions, Member States shall take into account their effectiveness and their cost relative to other possible preventive measures.

6.   Member States shall draw up and implement suitable monitoring programmes to assess the effectiveness of action programmes established pursuant to this Article.

Member States which apply Article 5 throughout their national territory shall monitor the nitrate content of waters (surface waters and groundwater) at selected measuring points which make it possible to establish the extent of nitrate pollution in the waters from agricultural sources.

7.   Member States shall review and if necessary revise their action programmes, including any additional measures taken pursuant to paragraph 5, at least every four years. They shall inform the Commission of any changes to the action programmes.

Article 6

1.   For the purpose of designating and revising the designation of vulnerable zones, Member States shall:

a) within two years of notification of the Directive, monitor the nitrate concentration in freshwaters over a period of one year:

    i) at surface water sampling stations, laid down in Article 5 (4) of Directive 75/440/EEC and/or at other sampling stations which are representative of surface waters of Member States, at least monthly and more frequently during flood periods;

    ii) at sampling stations which are representative of the groundwater aquifers of Member States, at regular intervals and taking into account the provisions of Directive 80/778/EEC;

b) repeat the monitoring programme outlined in (a) at least every four years, except for those sampling stations where the nitrate concentration in all previous samples has been below 25 mg/l and no new factor likely to increase the nitrage content has appeared, in which case the monitoring programme need be repeated only every eight years;

c) review the eutrophic state of their fresh surface waters, estuarial and coastal waters every four years.

2.   The reference methods of measurement set out in Annex IV shall be used.

Article 7

Guidelines for the monitoring referred to in Article 5 and 6 may be drawn up in accordance with the procedure laid down in Article 9.

Article 8

The Annexes to this Directive may be adapted to scientific and technical progress in accordance with the procedure laid down in Article 9.

Article 9

1.   The Commission shall be assisted by a Committee composed of the representative of the Member States and chaired by the representative of the Commission.

2.   The representative of the Commission shall submit to the Commission a draft of the measures to be taken. The Committee shall deliver its opinion on the draft within a time limit which the chairman may lay down according to the urgency of the matter. The opinion shall be delivered by the majority laid down in Article 148 (2) of the EEC Treaty in the case of decisions which the Council is required to adopt a proposal from the Commission. The votes of the

representatives of the Member States within the Committee shall be weighted in the manner set out in that Article. The chairman shall not vote.

3.
   a) the Commission shall adopt the measures envisaged if they are in accordance with the opinion of the Committee.

   b) If the measures envisaged are not in accordance with the opinion of the Committee, or if no opinion is delivered, the Commission shall, without delay, submit to the Council a proposal relating to the measures to be taken. The Council shall act by a qualified majority.

   c) If, on the expiry of a period of three months from the date of referral to the Council, the Council has not acted, the proposed measures shall be adopted by the Commission, save where the Council has decided against the said measures by a simple majority.

Article 10

1.   Member States shall, in respect of the four-year period following the notification of this Directive and in respect of each subsequent four-year period, submit a report to the Commission containing the information outlined in Annex V.

2.   A report pursuant to this Article shall be submitted to the Commission within six months of the end of the period to which it relates.

Article 11

On the basis of the information received pursuant to Article 10, the Commission shall publish summary reports within six months of receiving the reports from Member States and shall communicate them to the European Parliament and to the Council. In the light of the implementation of the Directive, and in particular the provisions of Annex III, the Commission shall submit to the Council by 1 January 1998 a report accompanied where appropriate by proposals for revision of this Directive.

Article 12

1.   The Member States shall bring into force the laws, regulations and administrative provisions necessary to

comply with this Directive within two years of its notification[1]. They shall forthwith inform the Commission thereof.

2.   When Member States adopt these measures, they shall contain a reference to this Directive or shall be accompanied by such reference on the occasion of their official publication. The methods of making such a reference shall be laid down by the Member States.

3.   Member States shall communicate to the Commission the texts of the provisions of national law which they adopt in the field governed by this Directive.

Article 13

This Directive is addressed to the Member States.

Done at Brussels, 12 December 1991.

For the Council

The President

J.G.M. ALDERS

---

[1]   This Directive was notified to the Member States on 19 December 1991.

ANNEX I

CRITERIA FOR IDENTIFYING WATERS REFERRED TO IN ARTICLE 3 (1)

A.   Waters referred to in Article 3 (1) shall be identified making use, inter alia, of the following criteria:

1)   whether surface freshwaters, in particular those used or intended for the abstraction of drinking water, contain or could contain, if action pursuant to Article 5 is not taken, more than the concentration of nitrates laid down in accordance with Directive 75/440/EEC;

2)   whether groundwaters contain more than 50 mg/l nitrates or could contain more than 50 mg/l nitrates if action pursuant to Article 5 is not taken;

3)   whether natural freshwater lakes, other freshwater bodies, estuaries, coastal waters and marine waters are found to be eutrophic or in the near future may become euthropic if action pursuant to Article 5 is not taken.

B.   In applying these criteria, Member States shall also take account of:

1)   the pyhsical and environmental characteristics of the waters and land;

2)   the current understanding of the behaviour of nitrogen compounds in the environment (water and soil);

3)   the current understanding of the impact of the action taken pursuant to Article 5.

ANNEX II

CODE(S) OF GOOD AGRICULTURAL PRACTICE

A.   A code or codes of good agricultural practice with the objective of reducing pollution by nitrates and taking account of conditions in the different regions of the Community should certain provisions covering the following items, in so far as they are relevant:

1)   periods when the land application of fertilizer is inappropriate;

2)   the land application of fertilizer to steeply sloping ground;

3)   the land application of fertilizer to water-saturated, flooded, frozen or snow-covered ground;

4)   the conditions for land application of fertilizer near water courses;

5)   the capacity and construction of storage vessels for livestock manures, including measures to prevent water pollution by run-off and seepage into the groundwater and surface water of liquids containing livestock manures and effluents from stored plant materials such as silage;

6)   procedures for the land application, including rate and uniformity of spreading, of both chemical fertilizer and livestock manure, that will maintain nutrient losses to water at an acceptable level.

B.   Member States may also include in their code(s) of good agricultural practices the following items:

7)   land use management, including the use of crop rotation systems and the proportion of the land area devoted to permanent crops relative to annual tillage crops;

8)   the maintenance of a minimum quantity of vegetation cover during (rainy) periods that will take up the nitrogen from the soil that could otherwise cause nitrate pollution of water;

9)   the establishment of fertilizer plans on a farm-by-farm basis and the keeping of records on fertilizer use;

10)   the prevention of water pollution from run-off and the downward water movement beyond the reach of crop roots in irrigation systems.

ANNEX III

MEASURES TO BE INCLUDED IN ACTION PROGRAMMES AS REFERRED TO IN ARTICLE 5 (4) (a)

1.   The measures shall include rules relating to:

1) periods when the land application of certain types of fertilizer is prohibited;

2) the capacity of storage vessels for livestock manure; this capacity must exceed that required for storage throughout the longest period during which land application in the vulnerable zone is prohibited, except where it can be demonstrated to the competent authority that any quantity of manure in excess of the actual storage capacity will be disposed of in a manner which will not cause harm to the environment;

3) limitation of the land application of fertilizers, consistent with good agricultural practice and taking into account the characteristics of the vulnerable zone concerned, in particular:

a) soil conditions, soil type and slope;

b) climatic conditions, rainfall and irrigation;

c) land use and agricultural practices, including crop rotation systems;

and to be based on a balance between:

i) the foreseeable nitrogen requirements of the crops,

and

ii) the nitrogen supply to the crops from the soil and from fertilization corresponding to:

- the amount of nitrogen present in the soil at the moment when the crop starts to use it to a significant degree (outstanding amounts at the end of winter),

- the supply of nitrogen through the net mineralization of the reserves of organic nitrogen in the soil,

- additions of nitrogen compounds from livestock manure,

- additions of nitrogen compounds from chemical and other fertilizers.

2.   These measures will ensure that, for each farm or livestock unit, the amount of livestock manure applied to the land each year, including by the animals themselves, shall not exceed a specified amount per hectare.

The specified amount per hectare be the amount of manure containing 170 kg N. However:

a) for the first four year action programme Member States may allow an amount of manure containing up to 210 kg N;

b) during and after the first four year action programme, Member States may fix different amounts from those referred to above. These amounts must be fixed so as not to prejudice the achievement of the objectives specified in Article 1 and must be justified on the basis of objectives criteria, for example:

   - long growing seasons,

   - crops with high nitrogen uptake,

   - high net precipitation in the vulnerable zone,

   - soils with exceptionally high denitrification capacity.

If a Member State allows a different amount under subparagraph (b), it shall inform the Commission which will examine the justification in accordance with the procedure laid down in Article 9.

3.   Member States may calculate the amounts referred to in paragraph 2 on the basis of animal numbers.

4.   Member States shall inform the Commission of the manner in which they are applying the provisions of paragraph 2. In the light of the information received, the Commission may, if it considers necessary, make appropriate proposals to the Council in accordance with Article 11.

ANNEX IV

REFERENCE METHODS OF MEASUREMENT

Chemical fertilizer

Nitrogen compounds shall be measured using the method described in Commission Directive 77/535/EEC of 22 June 1977 on the approximation of the laws of the Member States relating to methods of sampling and analysis for fertilizers[1], as amended by Directive 89/519/EEC[2].

Freshwaters, coastal waters and marine waters

Nitrate concentration shall be measured in accordance with Article 4a (3) of Council Decision 77/795/EEC of 12 December 1977 establishing a common procedure for the exchange of information on the quality of surface fresh water in the Community[3], as amended by Decision 86/574/EEC[4].

---

[1]   OJ No L 213, 22. 8. 1977, p. 1.
[2]   OJ No L 265, 12. 9. 1989, p. 30.
[3]   OJ No L 334, 24. 12. 1977, p. 29.
[4]   OJ No L 335, 28. 11. 1986, p. 44.

ANNEX V

INFORMATION TO BE CONTAINED IN REPORTS TO IN ARTICLE 10

1)   A statement of the preventive action taken pursuant to Article 4.

2)   A map showing the following:

   a)   waters identified in accordance with Article 3 (1) and Annex I indicating for each water which of the criteria in Annex I was used for the purpose of identification;

   b)   the location of the designed vulnerable zones, distinguishing between existing zones and zones designated since the previous report.

3)   A summary of the monitoring results obtained pursuant to Article 6, including a statement of the considerations which led to the designation of each vulnerable zone and to any revision of or addition to designations of vulnerable zones.

4)   A summary of the action programmes drawn up pursuant to Article 5 and, in particular:

   a)   the measures required by Article 5 (4) (a) and (b);

   b)   the information required by Annex III (4);

   c)   any additional measures or reinforced actions taken pursuant to Article 5 (5);

   d)   a summary of the results of the monitoring programmes implemented pursuant to Article 5 (6);

   e)   the assumptions made by the Member States about the likely timescale within which the waters identified in accordance with Article 3 (1) are expected to respond to the measure in the action programme, along with an indication of the level of uncertainty incorporated in these assumptions.

COUNCIL RESOLUTION 92/C 59/02[1]
of 25 February 1992
on the future Community groundwater policy

THE COUNCIL OF THE EUROPEAN COMMUNITIES,

UNDERLINES the vital importance of groundwater for all forms of life, for human health, and for safeguarding ecosystems;

STATES its concern about the lowering of groundwater levels and/or the pollution of certain aquifers;

NOTES that this important resource is limited, that its conservation for the future is a major political, economic and environmental imperative and that it can be exploited only in strict observance of the principle of sustainable development;

OBSERVES that freshwater management policy can be conducted only through coordinated action by all agents in the public and private sectors, taking due account of the principle of subsidiarity;

TAKES NOTE of the final declaration of the Ministerial Seminar held on 26 and 27 November 1991 on the future Community groundwater policy;

CALLS UPON THE COMMISSION:

— to submit, if possible by the middle of 1993, a detailed action programme for which that declaration may provide guidelines,

— to draft a proposal for revising Council Directive 80/68/EEC of 17 December 1979 on the protection of groundwater against pollution caused by certain dangerous substances by incorporating it into a general freshwater management policy, including freshwater protection;

REQUESTS the competent authorities and groups involved to contribute to the conservation of this natural resource in the areas under their control.

---

[1] OJ No C 59, 6. 3. 1992, p. 2.

COMMISSION DECISION 92/316/EEC[1]
of 11 March 1992
concerning aid envisaged by the Netherlands Government in favour of an environmentally-sound disposal of manure
(Only the Dutch text is authentic)

THE COMMISSION OF THE EUROPEAN COMMUNITIES,

Having regard to the Treaty establishing the European Economic Community, and in particular the first subparagraph of Article 93 (2) thereof,

Having in accordance with the abovementioned Articles, given notice to the parties concerned to submit their comments to it,

Whereas:

I

The Netherlands Government intends to institute an aid scheme for stimulating an environmentally-acceptable disposal of surplus manure (stimulering milieuhygiënisch verantwoorde afzet van mestoverschotten). This scheme, which is to be financed entirely with the yield of a levy to be paid by animal husbandry units who produce more manure than their land can take (i.e. more than 125 kg phosphates per hectare per annum), will finance the activities of the public foundation national manure bank (Stichting Landelijke Mestbank - SLM) in regions where there is a concentration of such units. The SLM as the statutory task of disposing of surplus manure in an environmentally-acceptable manner.

The nature of the environmental damage which may be caused by the inappropriate disposal of animal manure comes under many headings. These include contamination of surface and subterranean water supplies, gaseous emissions and residual heavy metals, through to bacteriological and aesthetic aspects. Whether or not environmental damage will be caused by the disposal of animal manure depends critically upon the conditions under which the disposal takes place, in terms of methods, timing and quantities.

By letter dated 8 April 1991 the Netherlands Government notified the Commission, pursuant to Article 93 (3) of the Treaty, of its intentions.

---

[1] OJ No L 170, 25. 6. 1992, p. 34.

After a first examination of the notification, the Commission considered that the aid was likely to distort competition and affect trade between Member States by favouring certain animal farmers in the Netherlands. The Commission noted that the description of activities to be financed by the SLM was not very clear, but that these would seem to concern transportation, storage and price regulation for manure disposal.

In so far as the aid would be used to supply manure processing factories with manure, aid would seem to be granted to those factories as well. The Commission also took into consideration that it had previously-accepted two other manure aid schemes in the Netherlands: an aid scheme for the distribution of high quality manure with decreasing aid intensities until its expiration in 1995 and an aid scheme in favour of the construction of some 20 manure processing factories in 1990 to 1994[1].

The Commission concluded that the aid scheme for stimulating an environmentally-acceptable disposal of surplus manure would seem to involve operation aid, to which in principle none of the derogations in Article 92 can apply. Furthermore, the new aid scheme would seem to be incompatible with the conditions under which the Commission had approved the two previous schemes referred to above. The degressivity and the date of expiration of the scheme for distributing high-quality manure would have no real significance if the new scheme were adopted. As for the manure processing factories, the Commission had based its approval on, among others, the Netherlands Government's assurance that no additional aid would be granted to these factories. The Commission's letter of approval dated 7 February 1991 had specifically noted this point and indicated the Commission's a priori negative attitude towards any further manure aid in the Netherlands. The Commission therefore decided to initiate the procedure laid down in Article 93 (2) of the Treaty.

The Netherlands Governement was informed of this decision by letter dated 4 June 1991 and was invited to provide its comments within one month. The other Member States and interested third parties were also given notice to submit their comments[2].

II

Within the framework of the procedure the Netherlands Government submitted observations by letters dated 5 July 1991, in bilateral meetings on 7 October and 17 October 1991 and by letter dated 18 November 1991. The Netherlands Government explained the operations of the manure bank SLM and the way these would be financed by means of levies and tariffs. The Netherlands Gov-

---

[1] OJ No C 82, 27. 3. 1991, p. 3.
[2] OJ No C 189, 20. 7. 1991, p. 5.

ernment accepted that the scheme had to be assessed by the Commission on the basis of Article 92 of the Treaty, but believed that there would be no distortion of competition, nor an effect on trade, given that the scheme would be financed entirely by means of a levy paid by animal husbandry units. In this context, the Netherlands Government also held that the scheme respected the 'polluter pays principle_ and claimed that the draft scheme in question would not entail additional aid to manure processing factories, nor would it serve to prolong the existing aid scheme for transporting high quality manure. With its latest letter, the Netherlands Government submitted the SLM's budget for 1992, which it had adapted in order to meet the Commission's concerns regarding the types of activity to be aided under the scheme.

Within the framework of the procedure, observations were also submitted by the Danish Government, by the European fertilizer manufacturers association EFMA, by the Italian federation of pig-breeders, by a German agricultural organization and by five individual manure processors in the Netherlands, Belgium and France. These observations were submitted to the Netherlands Government for its comments by letter dated 29 August 1991. The Netherlands Government submitted such comments by letter dated 7 October 1991.

III

The cost of an environmentally-sound disposal of the waste an economic operator produces is basically an element of his production cost. Animal husbandry units having an economic advantage through intensive production methods and relatively low transportation cost for feed due to their being concentrated in certain regions, must also bear the cost of an environmentally-sound disposal of their manure, in accordance with the polluter pays principle and Article 130r[1] of the Treaty, especially the principle that the polluter must pay. In the same way as the cost of production and profits are different for every individual operator, the cost of manure disposal will also differ, depending among others on the availability of and distance to potential outlets, such as land that can take additional manure or processing facilities.

Consequently the provision of public funds to the manure bank SLM in order to finance certain of its operations constitutes a type of State aid. The fact that these funds are raised by means of a levy on the production of surplus manure does not alter this appraisal. In the present case the levy is introduced by a regulation of the Landbouwschap (Agricultural Board), i.e. as an obligatory measure under public law; payment of the levy can be enforced. In its judgment of 11 November 1987 in Case 259/85 (2), the Court of Justice stated that the mere fact that a system of subsidies which benefits certain companies

---

[1]   France v. Commission, (1987) ECR 4418, paragraph 23.

in a specific sector is financed by a parafiscal charge levied on every supply of national goods in that sector is not sufficient to divest the system of its character as aid granted by a Member State within the meaning of Article 92 of the Treaty.

The rate of levy on surplus manure is fixed annually by the Landbouwschap. In doing so the Landbouwschap takes into account several factors: whether there is a regional surplus of manure, the type of manure produced and the magnitude of surplus production at farm level. For example, in 1992 the levy on surplus pig manure in the east of the Netherlands will be Hfl 3,23 per tonne, in the south of the Netherlands Hfl 3,69 per tonne and in the rest of the Netherlands nil.

The yield is in the first place used to cover the fixed cost (infrastructure and overheads) of the manure banks, in the second place their variable operation cost. The remainder of its operation cost is financed by means of tariffs paid by those units that actually supply manure to the SLM. Of the Hfl 71,6 million total expenditure the SLM is expected to have in 1992, Hfl 40 million will be covered by levies, Hfl 31,5 million by means of tariffs.

The effect of the proposed aid scheme will be to partly harmonize the cost of manure disposal, and therefore part of the production cost of animal husbandry units, by means of the levy. A second effect of the scheme will be an increasing willingness of manure producers to deliver their surplus manure to the SLM rather than to dispose of it through direct contacts with owners of land elsewhere, given that they will in any case have to finance part of the cost of the SLM, whether they use that manure bank or not.

In so far as the yield of the levy is used to finance part of the cost of supplying processing factories with manure, the aid is likely to favour these factories as well. The scheme will enable the SLM to create storage facilities and to regulate the supply of manure and the price at which it is offered to processing factories, thus limiting their normal entrepreneurial risk. Even though the Netherlands Government in its letter dated 5 July 1991 denied that the objective of the scheme was to grant additional aid to manure processing factories and stressed that the SLM will negotiate with these factories on a commercial basis in order to determine the quantities of manure that will be delivered and the price thereof, the Commission holds that the effect of the aid to the SLM will be to absorb part of the risk manure processing factories would normally have to bear. In this context the Commission notes that the Dutch delegation at the meeting held on 17 October 1991 recognized that the proposed scheme will have the effect of speeding up the construction of large-scale manure processing plants, so that these will be available when needed.

IV

There is competition between animal farmers in the Community and animals and their meat are traded between Member States. The Dutch animal husbandry sector accounts for an important part of Community production. In 1989 15 % of pork production in the Community, 9,2 % of egg production and 7,2 % of poultry production took place in the Netherlands.

In 1988 the Netherlands exported 759 049 tonnes of pigmeat (CN code 0203) to other Member States, in 1989 751 252 tonnes and in 1990 761 772 tonnes, which represented almost 50% of the totality of intra-Community trade in these products. In those years the Netherlands imported 24 214 tonnes, 16 747 tonnes and 22 227 tonnes respectively from other Member States.

In 1988 the Netherlands exported 365 938 tonnes of eggs (CN code 040700) to other Member States, in 1989 370 523 tonnes and in 1990 373 930 tonnes, which represented approximately 75 % of the totality of intra-Community trade in these products. In those years the Netherlands imported 9 407 tonnes, 13 253 tonnes and 19 556 tonnes respectively from other Member States.

In 1988 the Netherlands exported 218 480 tonnes of poultry meat (CN code 0207) to other Member States, in 1989 221 937 tonnes and in 1990 248 793 tonnes, which represented 40 to 45 % of the totality of intra-Community trade in these products. In those years the Netherlands imported 46 365 tonnes, 48 755 tonnes and 52 043 tonnes respectively from other Member States.

Manure processing is one of the four mechanisms with which the Netherlands Government intends to prevent and to dispose of surplus manure. The other mechanisms are: prohibition of expansion of manure production in units which already produce more manure that their land can take; reduction of manure production and minerals in manure by using appropriate feeds; distribution of manure inside the Netherlands.

In 1989 there was processing capacity available in the Netherlands for 420 000 tonnes of manure per annum. The environmental targets set by the Netherlands Government make it necessary to have processing capacity for 6 million tonnes per annum by the end of 1994 and for 20 million tonnes per annum by the year 2000. These ambitious targets call for the building of up to 20 large-scale processing plants with capacities of 250 000 to 500 000 tonnes per year before 1995.

Processed animal manure contains N, P and K in proportions similar to those in chemical fertilizers, but in lower concentrations (6 % - 6 % - 6 %). Its content of organic matter is, however, much higher. This organic matter improves the soil structure and the soil's ability to absorb water and minerals.

Notably in a warm and dry climate, organic fertilizers used over a longer period have been shown to lead to significantly higher crop yields.

When used as a fertilizer, manure competes with other organic fertilizers. According to a study made for the responsible Dutch Ministry in 1990 on the sales potential in other countries for Dutch processed animal manure[1], this product will compete with local animal manure, fish-meal, bone-meal, milled seed-waste, compost and sewage sludge. The potential market for processed animal manure depends in the first place on the price at which it is offered. According to the study referred to above, potential markets can be found inside the Community in France and in Spain and to a lesser extent in Portugal, Italy and Greece and in third countries such as the USA, Japan and Canada.

Depending on soil and crops, processed animal manure may also be in competition with chemical fertilizers. In a study paper on animal manure in Europe dated September 1991, EFMA calculated that if 50 % of the total one million tonnes of nitrogen coming from animal husbandry based on imported feedstuff were to be processed, the use of nitrogen from animal manure would rise by 100 000 tonnes, which represents about 1 % of the total sale of nitrogen fertilizer in Europe in 1988. In the paper EFMA assumed, however, that processing on such a scale would not take place, because the costs to the farmers would be prohibitive.

There is trade between Member States in animal and vegetable fertilizers, whether or not mixed together or chemically treated (CN code 3101). In 1988 the Netherlands exported 160 877 tonnes to other Member States, in 1989 210 170 tonnes and in 1990 253 182 tonnes, mainly to the Belgium-Luxembourg Economic Union, Germany and France, which represented 44 to 60 % of the totality of intra-Community trade in these products. In those years the Netherlands imported 44 404 tonnes, 37 357 tonnes and 65 994 tonnes respectively from other Member States. Dutch exports of processed animal manure to other Member States and to third countries can be expected to increase markedly if the planned processing plants are built.

Intensive, concentrated animal husbandry exists not only in the Netherlands, but also in other Member States, especially Belgium, France, Germany and Italy. In order to cope with the associated environmental problems, Council Directive 91/676/EEC of 12 December 1991 concerning the protection of waters against pollution caused by nitrate from agricultural sources[2] requires all Member States to take measures in order to dispose of their manure surplus in an environmentally-sound manner. There will consequently be increased

---

[1] Booz-Allen & Hamiltion : Afzetmogelijkheden voor verwerkte dierlijke mest, Den Haag 1990.
[2] OJ No L 375, 31. 12. 1991, p. 1.

competition between suppliers of manure, processed or not, in the Community and some replacement of chemical fertilizers by organic fertilizers.

Where financial aid strengthens the position of certain undertakings compared with others that are competing with them in the Community, such aid must be deemed to affect competition with such other undertakings. The measures envisaged may well increase competition from Dutch intensive animal husbandry and from processed manure.

Consequently, the aid which the Netherlands Government intends to grant to an environmentally-sound disposal of surplus manure affects trade between Member States and distorts competition between animal-farmers within the meaning of Article 92 (1) of the Treaty. In so far as the surplus manure in question is processed in order to be brought on the market as a dry organic fertilizer, the aid is also likely to distort competition with other manufacturers of organic and chemical fertilizers.

Article 92 (1) of the Treaty lays down the principle that aid having certain characteristics which it specifies is incompatible with the common market.

The derogations from that principle which are set out in Article 92 (2) of the Treaty are inapplicable in this instance, given the nature and objectives of the aid, and were not in any case invoked by the Netherlands Government.

V

Article 92 (3) of the Treaty specifies the aid which may be considered to be compatible with the common market. Compatibility with the Treaty must be viewed in the context of the Community and not of a single Member State. So as to maintain the proper functioning of the common market and take account of the principles laid down in Article 3 (f) of the Treaty, the derogations to the principle of Article 92 (1) which are set out in Article 92 (3) must be interpreted strictly in examining any aid scheme or any individual aid measure.

In particular, the derogations may be applied only if the Commission finds that, if the aid were not granted, market forces alone would not be sufficient to induce the recipients to act in such a way as to achieve one of the objectives pursued.

Applying the derogations to cases which do not contribute to such an objective, or where the aid is not necessary for this purpose, would mean conferring undue advantages on the industries or undertakings of certain Member States, whose financial position would be strengthened, and affecting trading conditions between Member States and distorting competition, without any justification based on the common interest referred to in Article 92 (3).

With regard to the derogations provided for in Article 92 (3) (a) and (c) for aid intended to promote or facilitate the promotion of certain regions, it should be noted that the standard of living in none of the regions of the Netherlands is abnormally low nor does one of the regions suffer from serious underemployment within the meaning of the derogation laid down in Article 92 (3) (a). Several regions in the Netherlands qualify for regional aid within the meaning of the derogation provided for in Article 92 (3) (c); these regions are mainly situated in the north of the Netherlands, whereas the manure problem is the largest in the south and the east. Moreover, the Netherlands Government has not claimed that the aid in question would serve to facilitate the development of certain regions.

With regard to the derogations provided for in Article 92 (3) (b), it is firstly to be noted that the aid is not intended to remedy a serious disturbance in the Dutch economy; nor, indeed, has the Netherlands Government put forward any argument calling for the application of this derogation. With respect to the derogations for aid to promote the execution of an important project of common European interest, the Commission has taken into consideration that the Community framework on State aids in environmental matters, of which all Member States were informed by letters dated 7 November 1974 and 7 July 1980, foresees that during a transitional period State aids designed to assist existing firms in adapting to laws or regulations imposing new major burdens relating to environmental protection will qualify for derogation under Article 92 (3) (b) of the Treaty, by being aids to promote the execution of an important project of common European interest. The framework specifies however that, in order to qualify for exemption under Article 92 (3) (b), national aids will have to be granted to finance investments necessary to the adaptation which the recipient firms will have to make to their plants in order to satisfy new major environmental obligations imposed by the State or the Community.

In the present case, the aid planned by the Netherlands Government is not designed to finance investments in animal husbandry units in order to comply with new environmental legislation, but on the contrary to allow manure producers to maintain their present production, by financing a new outlet for their surplus manure. The framework does not exclude environmental aids other than those it declares compatible with the common market; such other aids must then, however, qualify for the exemptions in Article 92 (3) (a) or (c).

With regard to the derogations provided for in Article 92 (3) (c) for aid to facilitate the development of certain economic activities, where such aid does not adversely affect trading conditions to an extent contrary to the common interest, the Commission notes that the aid scheme proposed by the Netherlands Government - even though it serves to maintain the present intensive, concentrated production structure of a large part of Dutch animal husbandry - can be said to facilitate its developments, by creating a system for an environmentally-sound disposal of its surplus manure. Having due regard to Article 130r of the Treaty the Commission notes that the environmental policy pursued by the Netherlands Government, in so far as it reduces manure pollution, is in the interest of the Community as a whole.

When the Commission decided in December 1990 not to object to the Netherlands Government's intention to grant 35 % investment aid for the construction of large-scale manure processing plants until the end of 1994, it did so on the basis of the environmental considerations referred to above and the high commercial risk involved in large-scale manure processing. At the same time the Commission expressed its concerns that if these processing plants should turn out to be less profitable than expected, the Netherlands Government might be tempted to introduce a system of operating aid.

With regard to the aid scheme now proposed, the Commission has taken note of the Netherlands Government's reasoning that a central organization such as the SLM serves a useful purpose for the sector as a whole: the SLM is obliged to accept all manure offered to it, thus creating a controllable and environmentally-sound outlet for animal husbandry units that will find it increasingly difficult to dispose of their manure by other means. The Commission has also taken account of the argument presented by the Dutch delegation in the meeting held on 17 October 1991, that the necessary processing capacity will be available when it is needed, thanks to the scheme.

The Commission is of the opinion that the aid to be granted under the scheme Stimulering milieuhygiënisch verantwoorde afzet van mestoverschotten consists of two components:

First, the financing of the SLM's fixed costs (administrative apparatus, creation and maintenance of storage facilities) in order to have an organization available to all manure producers who may, at any given time, have a surplus of manure and no other outlet. It is the Commission's view that the SLM serves a useful purpose for the Dutch animal husbandry sector as a whole and the facilities it offers can therefore well be financed by means of a levy. The Commission has previously approved aid in other Member States to collective sectoral activities financed by means of quasi-fiscal levies on domestic production[1].

Secondly, as for the financing of the variable costs the SLM will increasingly have, that is the cost of transporting, storing and delivering manure to other areas in the Netherlands or to processing factories, it is the Commission's view that these variable costs should eventually be entirely covered by the tariffs that manure producers who actually use the SLM as an outlet have to pay. In

---

[1] e.g. 20th Competition Report, point 274.

the SLM's budget for 1992, its variable cost is only partially covered by tariffs and partly by the yield of the levy. If this situation was to become permanent, the Dutch authorities could well grant operating aid to manure processing factories via the SLM, once these factories have been built, for their exploitation and for their export of processed manure to other Member States. Such operating aid would adversely affect trading conditions to an extent contrary to the common interest, to the detriment of other suppliers of fertilizers.

The second component of the aid proposed by the Netherlands Government can therefore not be allowed to continue to be granted after the initial period in which the first processing factories are to be built, that is the period until the end of 1994. The Netherlands Government itself has repeatedly stated that 35 % investment aid will only be necessary for the construction of the first large-scale processing factories to be built in this period, given the extraordinary risks involved in this stage.

Similarly, the use of part of the yield of the levy on surplus manure for financing other than infrastructural and overhead cost in the SLM can be considered to promote the creation of an environmentally-sound disposal mechanism for manure without adversely affecting trading conditions to an extent contrary to the common interest, if it remains limited to the initial period, in which the SLM has to start up its operations and manure producers will become acquainted with it, and if it is entirely financed by the sector itself.

VI

Conclusion: The scheme Stimulering milieuhygiënisch verantwoorde afzet van mestoverschotten involves aid fulfilling the tests set out in Article 92 (1) of the Treaty. The aid is completely financed by means of a levy imposed on the overproduction of manure. The aid to the fixed cost of the manure bank SLM can be considered compatible with the common market under Article 92 (3) (c). The aid to the variable cost of actually handling manure can only be considered compatible during the starting period ending on 31 December 1994. From 1 January 1995 on the latter aid cannot be granted. Reporting obligations will ensure verification that this condition is complied with,

HAS ADOPTED THIS DECISION:

Article 1

The aid entirely financed by means of a levy on manure surplus production, which the Netherlands intend to grant for stimulating an environmentally-acceptable disposal of surplus manure, can be considered compatible with the common market under Article 92 (3) (c) of the EEC Treaty, in so far as the aid does not exceed the fixed cost of the administrative apparatus and the creation and maintenance of storage facilities by the Stichting Landelijke Mestbank (SLM).

Article 2

The aid referred to in Article 1 can also be considered compatible with the common market if it covers part of the variable cost of the SLM in its starting period for manure disposal 1992 to 1994.

From 1 January 1995 on, however, such aid no longer meets the conditions for exception provided for in Article 92 (3) and therefore may not be granted after that date.

Article 3

The Netherlands shall submit annual reports on the operations of the SLM and the way these are financed, allowing the Commission to verify that this Decision is complied with.

Article 4

The Netherlands shall inform the Commission, within two months of the notification of this Decision, of the measures taken to comply with it.

Article 5

This Decision is addressed to the Kingdom of the Netherlands.

Done at Brussels, 11 March 1992.

For the Commission

Leon BRITTAN

Vice-President

COMMISSION DECISION 92/446/EEC[1]
of 27 July 1992
concerning questionnaires relating to directives in the water sector

THE COMMISSION OF THE EUROPEAN COMMUNITIES,

having regard to the Treaty establishing the European Economic Community,

Having regard to Council Directive 76/464/EEC of 4 May 1976 on pollution caused by certain dangerous substances discharged into aquatic environment of the Community[2], as amended by Directive 91/692/EEC of 23 December 1991 standardizing and rationalizing reports on the implementation of certain Directives relating to the environment[3], and in particular Article 13 (1) thereof, as well as the relevant provisions of the other Directives referred to in Annex I of Directive 91/692/EEC,

Having regard to Council Directive 75/440/EEC of 16 June 1975 concerning the quality required of surface water intended for the abstraction of drinking water in the Member States[4], as last amended by Directive 91/692/EEC, and in particular Article 9a thereof,

Having regard to Council Directive 80/778/EEC of 15 July 1980 relating to the quality of water intended for human consumption[5], as last amended by Directive 91/692/EEC, and in particular Article 17a thereof,

Having regard to Council Directive 76/160/EEC of 8 December 1975 concerning the quality of bathing water[6], as last amended by Directive 91/692/EEC, and in particular Article 13 thereof,

Whereas the Member States are required to draw up a report on the implementation of certain Community Directives on the basis of questionnaires or outlines drawn up by the Commission; whereas, according to Article 6 of Directive 91/692/EEC, these questionnaires or outlines are to be drawn up by the Commission assisted in this task by a committee composed of the repre-

---

[1] OJ No L 247, 27. 8. 1992, p. 10.
[2] OJ No L 129, 18. 5. 1976, p. 23.
[3] OJ No L 377, 31. 12. 1991, p. 48.
[4] OJ No L 194, 25. 7. 1975, p. 26.
[5] OJ No L 229, 30. 8. 1980, p. 11.
[6] OJ No L 31, 5. 2. 1976, p. 1.

sentatives of the Member States and chaired by the representatives of the Commission;

Whereas the measures envisaged by this Decision are in accordance with the opinion expressed by the aforementioned committee or were not the subject of an opinion of the committee within the time laid down by the chairman of the committee,

HAS ADOPTED THIS DECISION:

Article 1

The questionnaires contained in the Annex are hereby adopted.

Article 2

This Decision is addressed to the Member States.

Done at Brussels, 27 July 1992.

For the Commission

Karel VAN MIERT

Member of the Commission

ANNEX

LIST OF OUTLINES[1]

I.   Outline of the questionnaire on the following Directives:

—   Council Directive 76/464/EEC of 4 May 1976 on pollution caused by certain dangerous substances discharged into the aquatic environment of the Community;

—   Council Directive 82/176/EEC of 22 March 1982 on limit values and quality objectives for mercury discharges by the chloralkali electrolysis industry[2];

—   Council Directive 83/513/EEC of 26 September 1983 on limit values and quality objectives for cadmium discharges[3];

—   ouncil Directive 84/156/EEC of 8 March 1984 on limit values and quality objectives for mercury discharges by sectors other than the chlor-alkali electrolysis industry[4];

—   Council Directive 84/491/EEC of 9 October 1984 on limit values and quality objectives for discharges of hexachlorocyclohexane[5] and

—   Council Directive 86/280/EEC of 12 June 1986 on limit values and quality objectives for discharges of certain dangerous substances included in list I of the Annex to Directive 76/464/EEC[6],

as last amended by Directive 91/692/EEC.

---

[1]   The details of the outlines are not included.
[2]   OJ No L 81 of 27. 3. 1982, p. 29.
[3]   OJ No L 291 of 24. 10. 1983, p. 1.
[4]   OJ No L 74 of 17. 3. 1984, p. 49.
[5]   OJ No L 274 of 17. 10. 1984, p. 11.
[6]   OJ No L 181 of 4. 7. 1986, p. 16.

II.   Outline of the questionnaire on Council Directive 78/659/EEC of 18 July 1978 on the quality of fresh waters needing protection or improvement in order to support fish life[1], as last amended by Directive 91/692/EEC.

III.   Outline of the questionnaire on Council Directive 78/176/EEC of 20 February 1978 on waste from the titanium dioxide industry, as amended by Directive 83/29/EEC[2], and last by Directive 91/692/EEC.

IV.   Outline of the questionnaire on Council Directive 79/923/EEC of 30 October 1979 on the quality required of shellfish waters[3], as last amended by Directive 91/692/EEC.

V.   Outline of the questionnaire on Council Directive 80/68/EEC of 17 December 1979 on the protection of groundwater against pollution caused by certain dangerous substances[4], as last amended by Directive 91/692/EEC.

VI.   A. Outline of the questionnaire on Council Directive 75/440/EEC of 16 June 1975 concerning the quality required of surface water intended for the abstraction of drinking water in the Member States, as last amended by Directive 91/692/EEC;

VI.   B. Outline of the questionnaire on Council Directive 79/869/EEC of 9 October 1979 concerning the methods of measurement and frequencies of sampling and analysis of surface water intended for the abstraction of drinking water in the Member States[5], as last amended by Directive 91/692/EEC.

VII.   Outline of the questionnaire on Council Directive 80/778/EEC of 15 July 1980 relating to the quality of water intended for human consumption, as last amended by Directive 91/692/EEC.

VIII.   Outline of the questionnaire on Council Directive 76/160/EEC of 8 December 1975 concerning the quality of bathing water, as last amended by Directive 91/692/EEC.

---

[1]   OJ No L 222 of 14. 8. 1978, p. 1.
[2]   OJ No L 54 of 25. 2. 1978, p. 19.
[3]   OJ No L 281 of 10. 11. 1979, p. 47.
[4]   OJ No L 20 of 26. 1. 1980, p. 43.
[5]   OJ No L 271 of 29. 10. 1979, p. 44.

COUNCIL DECISION 93/114/EEC[1]
of 15 February 1993
concerning the conclusion of the Protocol to the Convention of 8 October 1990 between the Governments of the Federal Republic of Germany and of the Czech and Slovak Federal Republic and the European Economic Community on the International Commission for the Protection of the Elbe

THE COUNCIL OF THE EUROPEAN COMMUNITIES,

Having regard to the Treaty establishing the European Economic Community, and in particular Article 130s thereof,

Having regard to the proposal from the Commission[2],

Having regard to the opinion of the European Parliament[3],

Having regard to the opinion of the Economic and Social Committee[4],

Whereas, by Decision 91/598/EEC[5], the Community approved the Convention on the International Commission for the Protection of the Elbe;

Whereas it is essential that the International Commission established by that Convention be given legal personality and capacity in order that it may carry out its tasks;

Whereas, to this end, a Protocol to the Convention was adopted in Magdeburg on 9 December 1991; whereas the Protocol has been signed on behalf of the Community;

Whereas it is therefore necessary that the Community approve the Protocol,

HAS DECIDED AS FOLLOWS:

---

[1]   OJ No L 45 , 23. 2. 1993, p. 25.
[2]   OJ No C 185, 22. 7. 1992, p. 14.
[3]   OJ No C 305, 23. 11. 1992.
[4]   OJ No C 287, 4. 11. 1992, p. 38.
[5]   OJ No L 321, 23. 11. 1991, p. 24.

Article 1

The Protocol to the Convention of 8 October 1990 between the Governments of the Federal Republic of Germany and of the Czech and Slovak Federal Republic and the European Economic Community on the International Commission for the Protection of the Elbe is hereby approved on behalf of the European Economic Community.

The text of the Protocol is attached hereto.

Article 2

The President of the Council will, on behalf of the European Economic Community, inform the Government of the Federal Republic of Germany, in its capacity as depositary State, that the preconditions for the entry into force of the Protocol have been fulfilled as far as the Community is concerned, in accordance with Article 2 of the Protocol.

Done at Brussels, 15 February 1993.

For the Council

The President

M. JELVED

PROTOCOL

to the Convention of 8 October 1990 between the Governments of the Federal Republic of Germany and the Czech and Slovak Federal Republic and the European Economic Community on the International Commission for the Protection of the Elbe

THE GOVERNMENTS OF THE FEDERAL REPUBLIC OF GERMANY AND THE CZECH AND SLOVAK FEDERAL REPUBLIC AND THE EUROPEAN ECONOMIC COMMUNITY,

Having regard to the Convention of 8 October 1990 on the International Commission for the Protection of the Elbe,

HAVE AGREED AS FOLLOWS:

Article 1

For the purpose of fulfilment of tasks conferred on it under the Convention, the Commission shall have legal capacity in accordance with the law obtaining at the place at which its Secretariat has its headquarters. It shall in particular have the capacity to conclude any contracts required to fulfil its tasks, to acquire and to dispose of immovable and movable property and to take part in legal proceedings. For this purpose, the Commission shall be represented by its chairman. The chairman may appoint a representative in accordance with the rules of procedure.

Article 2

This Protocol shall enter into force 30 days after the day on which all signatories have informed the Government of the Federal Republic of Germany as depository that any preconditions for the entry into force required by national laws have been fulfilled.

Done at Magdeburg, 9 December 1991.

In original copies in the German and Czech languages, each text being equally binding.

For the Government of the Federal Republic of Germany

For the Government of the Czech and Slovak Federal Republic

For the European Economic Community

COUNCIL REGULATION (EEC) No 1541/93[1]
of 14 June 1993
fixing the non-rotational set-aside rate referred to in
Article 7 of Regulation (EEC) No 1765/92

THE COUNCIL OF THE EUROPEAN COMMUNITIES,

Having regard to the Treaty establishing the European Economic Community,

Having regard to Council Regulation (EEC) No 1765/92 of 30 June 1992, establishing a support system for producers of certain arable crops[2], and in particular Article 7 (1) thereof,

Whereas the second subparagraph of Article 7 (1) of Regulation (EEC) No 1765/92 states that non-rotational set-aside may be permitted in return for a higher set-aside percentage rate than that required for rotational set-aside; whereas this percentage must ensure a reduction in production comparable to that resulting from rotational set-aside; whereas a scientific study of the comparative effectiveness, as regards production control, of the two types of set-aside, shows that a variation of five percentage points over the rate for rotational set-aside should enable the Community's objective to be obtained;

Whereas there are, in the Community, zones to be designated as vulnerable to the pollution of water by nitrates; whereas the protection of the waters in these areas or even in the whole of the territory of a Member State must comprise, when Council Directive 91/676/EEC of 12 December 1991 concerning the protection of waters against pollution caused by nitrates from agricultural sources [3]is applied, a compulsory scheme of limiting the use of fertilizers; whereas such a scheme may, under certain conditions, amount to a significant reduction in the use of fertilizers as compared with normal practice and thus afford additional guarantees as concerns the way in which production is controlled; whereas, at the same time, the fact of encouraging non-rotational set-aside to be carried out in these zones may make it easier to pursue the objectives of the said .Directive; whereas, as a result, it is appropriate to set the variation as compared with rotational set-aside at three points for these zones;

Whereas the various institutes which participated in the study took different hypotheses as their departure points in considering the influence of crop

---

[1] OJ No L 154, 25. 6. 1993, p. 1.No
[2] OJ No L 181, 1. 7. 1992, p. 12. Regulation as amended by Regulation (EEC) No 364/93 (OJ No L 42, 19. 2. 1993, p. 3)
[3] OJ No L 375, 31. 12. 1991, p. 1.

rotation on yield; whereas this study, conducted throughout one year, has not led to any definite conclusion on this important matter; whereas it is therefore necessary to envisage a more detailed study under better conditions; whereas this new study should be carried out on a sufficiently large surface area, without, however, jeopardizing the objective of production control; whereas a period of two years would be necessary to complete such a study; whereas in one Member State there exists an extreme case, both in terms of land which is to be entered into set-aside and in terms of the apparent difference in effectiveness between rotation and non-rotation, which means that the experiment should take place in that Member State; whereas, in order to ensure major participation in non-rotational set-aside, on the one hand, and to create the requisite conditions for the study, on the other, the additional rate should be lower than five points; whereas in this respect the said additional rate should be fixed at three points for each Member State in which, according to the latest available estimates, the area to be entered into set-aside will exceed 13 % of the base area in the first year; whereas the best estimates available are to be found in the preliminary draft budget for 1994;

Whereas the provisions of this Regulation do not affect the obligations imposed upon Member States by Directive 91/676/EEC,

HAS ADOPTED THIS REGULATION:

Article 1

1.   The percentage of non-rotational set-aside referred to in the second subparagraph of Article 7 (1) of Regulation (EEC) No 1765/92 shall be fixed at the level of the percentage of rotational set-aside referred to in the same Article, plus five percentage points.

2.   However, an increased rate of only three percentage points shall be authorized:

—   in the vulnerable zones referred to in Directive 91/676/EEC or in the whole of the territory of a Member State which chooses to apply there the action programmes provided for by the said Directive, on condition that a significant reduction, recognized as such by the Commission, in the use of fertilizers is applied there,

—   for land set-aside for the 1994/95 and 1995/96 marketing years in any Member State in which, according to the estimates of the preliminary draft budget for 1994, the area to be entered into set-aside in the first year of the scheme will exceed 3 % of the base area laid down by Regulation (EEC) No 845/93[1]

Article 2

1.   At the end of the 1995/96 marketing year, the Commission shall draw up a report concerning the effect on production of the application of the first indent of Article 1 (2), together with, should the need arise, appropriate proposals.

2.   During the period referred to in the second indent of Article 1 (2), the Commission shall carry out a study in order to ascertain the effects of rotation on yields in the Member States concerned. Should this study show that the three additional percentage points for the non-rotational set-aside do not afford the same guarantee in terms of production control as the rate adopted for rotational set-aside, the rate to be applied in the Member States for non-rotational set-aside as from the 1996/97 marketing year shall be increased on the basis of the results of this study within the limit of the rate referred to in Article 1 (1).

Article 3

The implementing rules for this Regulation, and in particular the definition of the concept of 'significant reduction' referred to in Article 1 (2) and the rate for the non-rotational set-aside applicable in the Member States referred to in the second indent of Article 1 (2) as from the 1996/97 marketing year, shall be adopted in accordance with the procedure referred to in Article 12 of Regulation (EEC) No 1765/92.

Article 4

This Regulation shall enter into force on the third day following its publication in the *Official Journal of the European Communities.*

This Regulation shall be binding in its entirety and directly applicable in all Member States.

Done at Luxembourg, 14 June 1993.

For the Council

The President

B. WESTH

---

[1]   OJ No L 88, 8. 4. 1993, p. 27.

COMMISSION DECISION 93/430/EEC[1]
of 28 June 1993
establishing the ecological criteria for the award of the Community eco-label to washing machines

THE COMMISSION OF THE EUROPEAN COMMUNITIES,

Having regard to the Treaty establishing the European Economic Community,

Having regard to Council Regulation (EEC) No 880/92 of 23 March 1992 on a Community eco-label award scheme[2], and in particular Article 5 thereof,

Whereas the first subparagraph of Article 5 (1) of Regulation (EEC) No 880/92 provides that the conditions for the award of the Community eco-label shall be defined by product group;

Whereas Article 10 (2) of Regulation (EEC) No 880/92 states that the environmental performance of a product shall be assessed by reference to the specific criteria for product groups;

Whereas the second subparagraph of Article 5 (1) of Regulation (EEC) No 880/92 provides further that product groups, the specific ecological criteria for each group and their respective periods of validity are to be established in accordance with the procedure laid down in Article 7 of that Regulation, following the consultation procedure provided for in Article 6 thereof;

Whereas in accordance with Article 6 of Regulation (EEC) No 880/92 the Commission has consulted the principal interest groups within a consultation forum;

Whereas the measures provided for in this Decision are in accordance with the opinion of the Committee set up pursuant to Article 7 of Regulation (EEC) No 880/92,

HAS ADOPTED THIS DECISION:

---

[1] OJ L 198, 7; 8; 1993, p. 35.
[2] OJ No L 99, 11. 4. 1992, p. 1.

Article 1

The product group to which this Decision relates is defined as:

> front and top loading washing machines sold to the general public, excluding twin tubs and washer dryers,

> (hereinafter referred to as 'the product group').

Article 2

The environmental performance of the product group shall be assessed by reference to the specific ecological criteria set out in the Annex.

Article 3

The definition of the product group and the specific ecological criteria for the product group shall be valid until 30 June 1996.

Article 4

This Decision is addressed to the Member States.

Done at Brussels, 28 June 1993.

For the Commission

Yannis PALEOKRASSAS

Member of the Commission

ANNEX

ECO-LABEL CRITERIA FOR WASHING MACHINES

A.   Key criteria

These criteria are based on the major environmental impacts as highlighted in the cradle-to-grave assessment. The threshold levels must all be achieved in order to qualify for an eco-label.

i)   *Energy consumption*

The machine must use less than or equal to 0,23 kWh of electrical energy per kg of washload in an IEC 456 test for a cotton wash without prewash at 60 °C using cold fill only.

The machine must use less than or equal to 0,11 kWh of electrical energy per kg of washload in an IEC 456 test for a cotton wash without prewash at 40 °C using cold fill only.

ii)   *Water consumption*

The machine must use less than or equal to 17 litres of water per kg of washold in an IEC 456 test for a cotton wash without prewash at either 60 or 40 °C.

iii)   *Detergent consumption*

The machine must lose less than or equal to 5 % of detergent in an IEC 456 test with the detergent added via the detergent drawer.

B.   Best practice criteria

Best practice criteria relate to features of a washing machine which make a smaller contribution to the overall environmental impact of the product. The qualifying levels for these criteria reflect best environmental practice. All of these criteria must be achieved in order to qualify for an eco-label.

i)   *User instructions*

1)   The machine must have clear markings on it identifying the settings appropriate according to fabric type and laundry code.

2)   The machine must have clear markings on it identifying energy and water saving programmes and options.

3)   Clear instructions must be made available to the consumer providing:

- advice to use a full load rather than part loads wherever possible,

- advice about the best wash temperature to use according to the fabric type,

- advice on varying the detergent dose according to water hardness, load size and the degree of soil,

- advice on the machine installation which makes the most appropriate use of the hot and cold fill, if available on the machine, including advice based on the fuel used for home water heating,

- advice on sorting fabrics appropriately,

- advice on situations where a prewash, if available, is likely to be required,

- information about the energy consumption and the water consumption of the machine for different temperature settings and for different load settings and according to whether hot and cold fill is an option,

- advice about the machine being made of materials which are recyclable and that it should be disposed of accordingly.

ii)   *Encouragement to recycling*

Where they occur in components in quantities greater than 50 g the following polymeric materials must have a permanent marking identifying the material:

- polypropylene,

- polystyrene,

- PVC,

- HDPE,

- LDPE,

- ABS,

- polyamide,

- other.

The marking must use the symbols or abbreviated terms given in ISO 1043.

C.   Performance criteria

i)   *Wash performance*

The machine must achieve at least a minimum of 20 % stain removal based on the carbon black soiled sample EMPA test cloth in an IEC 456 test at 60 °C.

The machine must achieve at least a minimum of 6 % stain removal based on the carbon black soiled sample EMPA test cloth in an IEC 456 test at 40 °C.

ii)   *Rinse efficiency*

The machine must achieve at least a minimum rinsing efficiency of 60 dilutions as defined in IEC 456.

COMMISSION DECISION 93/431/EEC[1]
of 28 June 1993
establishing the ecological criteria for the award of the Community eco-label to dishwashers

THE COMMISSION OF THE EUROPEAN COMMUNITIES,

Having regard to the Treaty establishing the European Economic Community,

Having regard to Council Regulation (EEC) No 880/92 of 23 March 1992 on a Community eco-label award scheme[2], and in particular Article 5 thereof,

Whereas the first subparagraph of Article 5 (1) of Regulation (EEC) No 880/92 provides that the conditions for the award of the Community eco-label shall be defined by product group;

Whereas Article 10 (2) of Regulation (EEC) No 880/92 states that the environmental performance of a product shall be assessed by reference to the specific criteria for product groups;

Whereas the second subparagraph of Article 5 (1) of Regulation (EEC) No 880/92 provides further that product groups, the specific ecological criteria for each group and their respective periods of validity are to be established in accordance with the procedure laid down in Article 7 of that Regulation, following the consultation procedure provided for in Article 6 thereof;

Whereas in accordance with Article 6 of Regulation (EEC) No 880/92 the Commission has consulted the principal interest groups within a consultation forum;

Whereas the measures provided for in this Decision are in accordance with the opinion of the Committee set up pursuant to Article 7 of Regulation (EEC) No 880/92,

HAS ADOPTED THIS DECISION:

---

[1] OJ No 198, 7. 8. 1993, p. 38.
[2] OJ No L 99, 11. 4. 1992, p. 1.

Article 1

The product group to which this Decision relates is defined as:

dishwashers sold to the general public,

(hereinafter referred to as 'the product group_).

Article 2

The environmental performance of the product group shall be assessed by reference to the specific ecological criteria set out in the Annex.

Article 3

The definition of the product group and the specific ecological criteria for the product group shall be valid until 30 June 1996.

Article 4

This Decision is addressed to the Member States.

Done at Brussels, 28 June 1993.

For the Commission

Yannis PALEOKRASSAS

Member of the Commission

ANNEX

ECO-LABEL CRITERIA FOR DISHWASHERS

A.   Key Criteria

These criteria are based on the major environmental impacts as highlighted in the cradle-to-grave assessment. The threshold levels must all be achieved in order to qualify for an eco-label.

i)   *Energy Consumption*

Standard size models (10 or more place settings)

The machine must use less than or equal to 0,125 kWh of electrical energy per place setting in an IEC 436 test.

Slimline and compact models (less than 10 place settings)

The machine must use less than or equal to 0,15 kWh of electrical energy per place setting in an IEC 436 test.

ii)   *Water Consumption*

Standard size models (10 or more place settings)

The machine must use less than or equal to 1,85 litres of water per place setting in an IEC 436 test.

Slimline and compact models (less than 10 place settings)

The machine must use less than or equal to 2,25 litres of water per place setting in an IEC 436 test.

B.   Best practice criteria

Best practice criteria relate to features of a dishwasher which make a smaller contribution to the overall environmental impact of the product. The qualifying levels for these criteria reflect best environmental practice. All of these criteria must be achieved in order to qualify for an eco-label.

i)   *User instructions*

1)   The machine must have clear markings on it identifying the settings appropriate according to the type of load (e.g. glass, china, pots and pans, crockery) and degree of soil.

2) Where dry heat boost is provided, it must be an option; it should not occur automatically.

3) On the machine there must be clear instructions to use a full load wherever possible.

4) Clear instructions must be made available to the consumer providing:

- advice on varying the detergent dosing according to the degree of soil,

- advice on varying the salt dosing according to water hardness,

- advice on the machine installation which makes the most appropriate use of the hot and cold fill, if available on the machine, including advice based on the fuel used for home water heating,

- advice to avoid rinsing items before placing them in the dishwater,

- advice on the best use of the rinse and hold option, if available,

- advice on the best use of the dry heat boost option, if available,

- information about the energy consumption of the machine for different programmes and with and without dry heat boost,

- information about the water consumption of the machine for different programmes and options,

- advice about te machine being made of materials which are recyclable and that it houd be disposed of accordingly.

ii) *Encouragement to recycling*

Where they occur in components in quantities greater than 50 g the following polymeric materials must have a permanent marking identifying the material:

- polypropylene,

- polystyrene,

- PVC,

- HDPE,

- LDPE,

- ABS,

- polyamide,

- other.

The marking must use the symbols or abbreviated terms given in ISO 1043.

C.   Performance criteria

i)   *Wash performance*

The machine must achieve at least a minimum wash efficiency of 85 % in an IEC 436 test.

ii)   *Drying efficiency*

The machine must achieve at least a minimum drying efficiency of 70 % in an IEC 436 test.

COMMISSION REGULATION (EEC) No 2158/93[1]
of 28 July 1993
concerning the application of amendments to the International Convention for the Safety of Life at Sea, 1974, and to the International Convention for the Prevention of Pollution from ships, 1973, for the purpose of Council Regulation (EEC) No 613/91

THE COMMISSION OF THE EUROPEAN COMMUNITIES,

Having regard to the Treaty establishing the European Economic Community,

Having regard to Council Regulation (EEC) No 613/91 of 4 March 1991 on the transfer of ships from one register to another within the Community[2], and in particular Article 1 (2) (a) thereof,

Whereas the applicability of the rules of the International Convention for the Safety of Life at Sea, 1974 (1974 Solas), and of the International Convention for the Prevention of Pollution from Ships, 1973, as amended by the 1978 Protocol (1973/78 Marpol), for the purpose of the transfer of ships is limited to those rules in force on the date of the adoption of Regulation (EEC) No 613/91, namely 4 March 1991;

Whereas in the meantime, due to the need to upgrade the safety standard of ships, the 1974 Solas and its 1978 Protocol were amended on 9 and 10 November 1988, 11 April 1989 and 23 May 1990; whereas such amendments came into force internationally on 1 February 1992;

Whereas in the meantime also, due to the need to upgrade the standards of prevention of pollution from ships, the 1973/78 Marpol was amended on 4 July 1991, which amendments came into force internationally on 4 April 1993;

Whereas, in order to ensure the application of these upgraded maritime safety and pollution prevention standards within the Community with regard to the transfer of ships between registers of Member States, these amendments should be declared applicable for the purposes of Regulation (EEC) No 613/91;

Whereas the measures provided for in this Regulation are in accordance with the opinion of 7 May 1993 of the Committee on Transfer of Ships,

---

[1] OJ No L 194, 3. 8. 1993, p. 5.
[2] OJ No L 68, 15. 3. 1991, p. 1.

HAS ADOPTED THIS REGULATION:

Article 1

The following amendments to the 1974 International Convention for the Safety of Life at Sea (1974 Solas) shall apply for the purpose of Council Regulation (EEC) No 613/91:

1) resolution 1 of the 'Conference of Contracting Governments to the International Convention for the Safety of Life at Sea 1974 on the Global Maritime Distress and Safety System', of 9 November 1988, amending Chapters I, II-1, III, IV, V, and the Appendix of the Annex to the 1974 Solas;

2) resolution 2 of the 'Conference of Contracting Governments to the International Convention for the Safety of Life at Sea 1974 on the Global Maritime Distress and Safety System', of 9 November 1988, adopting the records of equipment (Form E and R) to supplement the Solas Cargo Ship Safety Equipment Certificate and Cargo Ship Safety Radio Certificate as prescribed in the Annex to the 1974 Solas;

3) the resolution of the 'Conference of Parties to the Protocol of 1978 relating to the International Convention for the Life at Sea 1974 on the Global Maritime Distress and Safety System', of 10 November 1988, amending Chapter I and the Appendix thereto of the Annex to the Protocol of 1978 relating to the 1974 Solas;

4) resolution MSC 13 (57) of the 57th meeting of the Maritime Safety Committee of the International Maritime Organization, adopted on 11 April 1989, amending Chapters II-1, II-2, III, IV, V and VII of the Annex to the 1974 Solas;

5) resolution MSC 19 (58) of the 58th meeting of the Maritime Safety Committee of the International Maritime Organization, adopted on 23 May 1990, amending Chapter II-1 of the Annex to the 1974 Solas.

Article 2

Resolution MEPC 47 (31) of the 31st meeting of the Marine Environment Protection Committee of the International Maritime Organization of 4 July 1991, amending Annex I to the International Convention for the Prevention of Pollution from Ships, 1973, as amended by the 1978 Protocol, shall apply for the purposes of Regulation (EEC) No 613/91.

Article 3

This Regulation shall enter into force on the seventh day following its publication in the *Official Journal of the European Communities*.

This Regulation shall be binding in its entirety and directly applicable in all Member States.

Done at Brussels, 28 July 1993.

For the Commission

Abel MATUTES

Member of the Commission

COMMISSION DECISION 93/481/EEC[1]
of 28 July 1993
concerning formats for the presentation of national programmes as foreseen by Article 17 of Council Directive 91/271/EEC

THE COMMISSION OF THE EUROPEAN COMMUNITIES,

Having regard to the Treaty establishing the European Economic Community,

Having regard to Council Directive 91/271/EEC of 21 May 1991 concerning urban waste water treatment[2], and in particular Article 17 (4) thereof,

Whereas the Member States are required to draw up a report concerning their national programme for the implementation of Council Directive 91/271/EEC on the basis of formats drawn up by the Commission according to the procedure set out by Article 18 of this Directive;

Whereas, the measures envisaged by this Decision are in accordance with the opinion expressed by the Committee established by Article 18 of the said Directive,

HAS ADOPTED THIS DECISION:

Article 1

The formats contained in the Annex[3] are hereby adopted.

Article 2

This Decision is addressed to the Member States.

Done at Brussels, 28 July 1993.

For the Commission

Yannis PALEOKRASSAS

Member of the Commission

---

[1]   OJ No L 226, 7. 9. 1993, p. 23.
[2]   OJ No L 135, 30. 5. 1991, p. 40.
[3]   Not included.

COMMISSION DIRECTIVE 93/80/EEC[1]
of 23 September 1993
amending Council Directive 90/656/EEC on the transitional measures applicable in Germany with regard to certain Community provisions relating to the protection of the environment

THE COMMISSION OF THE EUROPEAN COMMUNITIES,

Having regard to the Treaty establishing the European Economic Community,

Having regard to Council Directive 90/656/EEC of 4 December 1990 on the transitional measures applicable in Germany with regard to certain Community provisions relating to the protection of the environment[2], and in particular Article 18 (6) thereof,

Whereas Directive 90/656/EEC lays down various time limits for putting certain Community rules on the environment into effect in the territory of the former German Democratic Republic;

Whereas the time limits specified in the said Directive were based on information on the rules in force and the state of the environment in the territory of the former German Democratic Republic which was found to be incomplete, approximative, uncertain and unreliable;

Whereas this results in a situation which is exceptional in all respects;

Whereas neither the Federal Republic of Germany nor the institutions of the European Communities were able, at the time of adoption of the said Directive, to foresee sufficiently clearly how the state of the environment would change in the territory of the former German Democratic Republic;

Whereas the said Directive for this reason provides for a simplified procedure by which the Commission, after obtaining the opinion of an ad hoc Committee, may authorize the extension to 31 December 1995 at the latest of the deadlines for putting certain Community rules on the environment laid down in the said Directive into effect in the territory of the former German Democratic Republic;

---

[1]   OJ No L 256, 14. 10. 1993, p. 32.
[2]   OJ No L 353, 17. 12. 1990, p. 59.

Whereas the degree of obsolescence of the industrial production units situated in the territory of the former German Democratic Republic, which discharge dangerous substances into the surface water, and the severity of the environmental damage attributable to those discharges have been found to be far in excess of the evaluations on the basis of which the date of 31 December 1992 was laid down in Directive 90/656/EEC for putting the Directives into effect;

Whereas it is therefore necessary to extend the deadlines laid down for the application of the said Directives to installations which were situated in the territory of the former German Democratic Republic at the time of German unification, in order to allow time for making the necessary changes to the said installations;

Whereas the measures provided for in this Directive are in conformity with the opinion expressed by the Committee referred to in Article 18 (4) of Directive 90/656/EEC,

HAS ADOPTED THIS DIRECTIVE:

Article 1

Article 3 of Directive 90/656/EEC is hereby amended as follows:

1.   Paragraph 1 is replaced by the following:

'1. .... By way of derogation from Directive 76/464/CEE[1], Directive 82/176/CEE[2], Directive 83/513/CEE[3], Directive 84/156/CEE[4], Directive 84/491/CEE[5], Directive 86/280/CEE[6] and Directive 88/347/CEE[7], the Federal Republic of Germany shall be authorized to apply, in respect of the territory of the former German Democratic Republic, the

---

[1]   OJ No L 129, 18. 5. 1976, p. 23.
See also Community Legislation concerning the environment, volume 1, General Policy, first edition.
[2]   OJ No L 81, 27. 3. 1982, p. 29.
See also Community Legislation concerning the environment, volume 7, Water, first edition.
[3]   OJ No L 291, 24. 10. 1983, p. 1.
See also Community Legislation concerning the environment, volume 7, Water, first edition.
[4]   OJ No L 74, 17. 3. 1984, p. 49.
See also Community Legislation concerning the environment, volume 7, Water, first edition.
[5]   OJ No L 274, 17. 10. 1984, p. 11.
See also Community Legislation concerning the environment, volume 7, Water, first edition.

provisions laid down in the said Directives to industrial installations which, on the date of German unification, were located in that territory, from 31 December 1995 at the latest.'

2.   Paragraph 4 is replaced by the following:

'4. The special programmes provided for in Article 4 of Directive 84/156/EEC and Article 5 of Directive 86/280/EEC shall be drawn up and put into effect by 31 December 1995 at the latest.'

Article 2

This Directive is addressed to the Member States.

Done at Brussels, 23 September 1993.

For the Commission

Yannis PALEOKRASSAS

Member of the Commission

---

6   OJ No L 181, 4. 7. 1986, p. 16.
    See also Community Legislation concerning the environment, volume 7, Water, first edition.
7   OJ No L 158, 25. 6. 1988, p. 35.
    See also Community Legislation concerning the environment, volume 7, Water, first edition.

COUNCIL DECISION 93/540/EEC[1]
of 18 October 1993
approving certain amendments to the Agreement for cooperation in dealing with pollution of the North Sea by oil and other harmful substances (Bonn Agreement)

THE COUNCIL OF THE EUROPEAN COMMUNITIES,

Having regard to the Treaty establishing the European Economic Community, and in particular Article 130s thereof,

Having regard to the proposal from the Commission[2],

Having regard to the opinion of the European Parliament[3],

Having regard to the opinion of the Economic and Social Committee[4],

Whereas by Decision 84/358/EEC[5] the Council approved on 28 June 1984 the Agreement for cooperation in dealing with pollution of the North Sea by oil and other harmful substances signed in Bonn on 13 September 1983;

Whereas at their first meeting held in Bonn from 19 to 22 September 1989 the Contracting Parties to the Agreement agreed on a number of amendments designed to include in the Agreement provisions concerning pollution surveillance activities, in order to ensure implementation of paragraphs 46 to 50 of the Ministerial Declaration adopted at the Second international conference for the protection of the North Sea held in London on 24 and 25 November 1987;

Whereas the Contracting Parties also decided to amend the demarcation zone of the Skagerrak, as set out in Article 2 (a) of the Agreement;

Whereas the amendments can come into force only when they have been approved by all the Contracting Parties, in accordance with Article 16 (2) of the Agreement,

HAS DECIDED AS FOLLOWS:

---

[1] OJ No L 263, 22. 10. 1993, p. 51.
[2] OJ No C 114, 5. 5. 1992, p. 13.
[3] OJ No C 42, 15. 2. 1993, p. 36.
[4] OJ No C 287, 4. 11. 1992, p. 1.
[5] OJ No L 188, 16. 7. 1984, p. 7.

Article 1

The amendments to the Agreement for cooperation in dealing with pollution of the North Sea by oil and other harmful substances, (Bonn Agreement) adopted by the Contracting Parties at their first meeting held in Bonn from 19 to 22 September 1989, are hereby approved on behalf of the European Economic Community.

The text of the Decision concerning these amendments is attached to this Decision.

Article 2

The President of the Council shall, on behalf of the European Economic Community, notify the Depositary Government referred to in Article 16 (2) of the Agreement of the adoption of the instrument of approval.

Done at Luxembourg, 18 October 1993.

For the Council

The President

A. BOURGEOIS

DECISION
of 22 September 1989
concerning amendments of the agreement

THE CONTRACTING PARTIES to the Agreement for Cooperation in Dealing with Pollution of the North Sea by Oil and Other Harmful Substances, done at Bonn on 13 September 1983 (hereinafter referred to as 'the Agreement');

RECALLING Article 1 of the Agreement for Cooperation in Dealing with Pollution of the North Sea by Oil and Other Harmful Substances, done at Bonn on 13 September 1983, according to which the Agreement shall apply whenever the presence or the prospective presence of oil or other harmful substances polluting or threatening to pollute the sea within the North Sea presents a grave and imminent danger to the coast or related interests of one or more Contracting Parties;

RECALLING paragraph XVI, subparagraphs 46 to 50 of the Ministerial Declaration of the Second International Conference on the Protection of the North Sea, held in London from 24-25 November 1987;

RECOGNIZING that the Agreement does not contain provisions referring to the use of surveillance as an aid to detecting pollution and to preventing violations of anti-pollution regulations;

DESIRING to extend the scope of the Agreement to such activities;

RECOGNIZING ALSO the need to adjust the southern geographical limit of the Skagerrak as defined in Article 2 of the Agreement;

HAVE AGREED to amend the Agreement as follows:

Article I

Article 1 of the Agreement shall be amended to read as follows:

'This Agreement shall apply:

1) whenever the presence or the prospective presence of oil or other harmful substances polluting or threatening to pollute the sea within the North Sea area, as defined in Article 2 of this Agreement, presents a grave and imminent danger to the coast or related interests of one or more Contracting Parties and

2) to surveillance conducted in the North Sea area as an aid to detecting and combating such pollution and to preventing violations of anti-pollution regulations.'

Article II

Article 2 of the Agreement shall be amended to read as follows:

'For the purpose of this Agreement the North Sea area means the North Sea proper southwards of latitude 61° N, together with:

a) the Skagerrak, the limit of which is determined east of the Skaw by the latitude 57° 44' 43'' N;

b) the English Channel and its approaches eastwards of a line drawn fifty nautical miles to the west of a line joining the Scilly Isles and Ushant.'

Article III

Article 3 of the Agreement shall be amended to read as follows:

'1. The Contracting Parties consider that the matters referred to in Article 1 of this Agreement call for active co-operation between them.

2. The Contracting Parties shall jointly develop and establish guidelines for the practical, operational and technical aspects of joint action and coordinated surveillance as referred to in Article 6A.'

Article IV

Article 4 of the Agreement shall be amended to read as follows:

'Contracting Parties undertake to inform the other Contracting Parties about:

a) their national organization for dealing with pollution of the kind referred to in Article 1 paragraph 1 of this Agreement, and for enforcing pollution regulations;

b) the competent authorities responsible for receiving and dispatching reports of such pollution and for dealing with questions concerning measures of mutual assistance and coordinated surveillance between Contracting Parties;

c) their national means for avoiding or dealing with such pollution, which might be made available for international assistance;

d) mew ways in which such pollution may be avoided and about new effective measures to deal with it;

e) major pollution incidents of this kind dealt with;

f) new developments in the technology of conducting surveillance;

g) their experience in the use of surveillance means and techniques in the detection of pollution and the prevention of violations of anti-pollution regulations, including use in cooperation with other Contracting Parties;

h) information of mutual interest derived from their surveillance activities;

i) their national programmes for surveillance, including cooperative arrangements with other Contracting Parties.'

Article V

A new Article 6A shall be added to the Agreement as follows:

'Surveillance shall be carried out, as appropriate, by the Contracting Parties in their zone of responsibility or zones of joint responsibility referred to in Article 6 of this Agreement. The Contracting Parties may bilaterally or multilaterally conclude agreements on or make arrangements for cooperation in the organization of surveillance in the whole or part of the zones of the Parties concerned.'

Article VI

Article 8 of the Agreement shall be amended to read as follows:

'1.   The provisions this Agreement shall not be interpreted as in any way prejudicing the rights and obligations of the Contracting Parties under international law, especially in the field of the prevention and combating of marine pollution.

2.   In no case shall the division into zones referred to in Article 6 of this Agreement be invoked as a precedent or argument in any matter concerning sovereignty or jurisdiction.

3.   The division into zones referred to in Article 6 of this Agreement shall in no way restrict the rights of Contracting Parties to carry out in accordance with international law surveillance activities beyond the limits of their zones._

Article VII

Article 9 of the Agreement shall be amended to read as follows:

'1.   In the absence of an agreement concerning the financial arrangements governing actions of Contracting Parties to deal with pollution which might be concluded on a bilateral or multilateral basis or on the occasion of a joint combating operation, Contracting Parties shall bear the costs of their respective actions in dealing with pollution in accordance with subparagraph (a) or subparagraph (b) below:

   a)   If the action was taken by one Contracting Party at the express request of another Contracting Party, the Contracting Party requesting such assistance shall reimburse to the assisting Contracting Party the costs of its action;

   b)   If the action was taken by a Contracting Party on its own initiative, this Contracting Party shall bear the costs of its action.

2.   The Contracting Party requesting assistance may cancel its request at any time, but in that case it shall bear the costs already incurred or committed by the assisting Contracting Party.

3.   Unless otherwise specified in bilateral or multilateral agreements or arrangements, each Contracting Party shall bear the costs of its surveillance activities carried out in accordance with Article 6A.'

Article VIII

The Contracting Parties shall notify the Depositary Government of their approval of these amendments in accordance with Article 16, paragraph 2 of the Agreement.

COUNCIL DECISION 93/550/EEC[1]
of 20 October 1993
concerning the conclusion of the cooperation agreement for the protection of the coasts and waters of the north-east Atlantic against pollution

THE COUNCIL OF THE EUROPEAN COMMUNITIES,

Having regard to the Treaty establishing the European Economic Community, and in particular Article 130s thereof,

Having regard to the proposal from the Commission[2],

Having regard to the opinion of the European Parliament[3],

Having regard to the opinion of the Economic and Social Committee[4],

Whereas the first two action programmes of the European Communities on the environment[5] emphasize the importance for the Community of dealing with pollution of the seas in general and make provision inter alia for Community measures to deal with pollution caused by transport and shipping; whereas they specify that the task of protecting sea water constitutes a matter of priority with a view to maintaining vital ecological balances;

Whereas the third action programme of the European Communities on the environment[6] emphasizes that, in the event of an accident, the authorities in the Member States concerned must be able to intervene quickly, in a coordinated manner and with sufficient means;

Whereas the fourth environmental action programme of the European Communities[7] confirms that the control of pollution from oil spills remains a valid priority and, indeed, that the priority attributed to marine pollution is increasing; whereas it recognizes that considerable attention must be paid to other dangerous substances transported by sea, as well as to oil;

---

[1] OJ No C 56, 26. 2. 1993, p. 13.
[2] OJ No C 56, 26. 2. 1993, p. 13.
[3] OJ No C 176, 28. 6. 1993, p. 211.
[4] OJ No C 201, 26. 7. 1993, p. 48.
[5] OJ No C 112, 20. 12. 1973, p. 1 and OJ No C 139, 13. 6. 1977, p. 1.
[6] OJ No C 46, 17. 2. 1983, p. 9.
[7] OJ No C 328, 7. 12. 1987, p. 23.

Whereas the fifth environmental action programme of the European Communities[1], on the one hand, refers to the need to improve the general state of preparation and capacity for intervention in the event of natural and technological disasters and, on the other, stresses the need to improve the means of intervention in view of the increased risks inherent in particular in dangerous transport operations, which in concrete terms involves improving and further upgrading mutual assistance procedures;

Whereas the Commission has participated, on behalf of the Community, in the negotiations to prepare an international cooperation agreement for the protection of the coasts and waters of the north-east Atlantic against pollution;

Whereas, as a result of those negotiations, the Cooperation Agreement for the protection of the coasts and waters of the north-east Atlantic against pollution was adopted on 17 October 1990 in Lisbon, and signed on behalf of the Community;

Whereas that Agreement fills a gap, as far as the north-east Atlantic is concerned, in international action relating to accidental marine pollution, the Baltic Sea, the North Sea and the Mediterranean Sea being already covered by multilateral agreements for cooperation in case of accidental marine pollution;

Whereas it is desirable for the Community to approve that Agreement in order to play its part in achieving its objectives alongside Member States, especially in consideration of Council Decision 86/85/EEC of 6 March 1986 establishing a Community information system for the control and reduction of pollution caused by the spillage of hydrocarbons and other harmful substances at sea or in major inland waters[2],

HAS DECIDED AS FOLLOWS:

Article 1

The Cooperation Agreement for the protection of the coasts and waters of the north-east Atlantic against pollution, as adopted in Lisbon on 17 October 1990, is hereby approved on behalf of the European Economic Community.

The text of the Agreement is attached to this Decision.

---

[1] OJ No C 138, 17. 5. 1993, p. 33.
[2] OJ No L 77, 22. 3. 1986, p. 33. Decision as amended by Decision 88/346/EEC (OJ No L 158, 25. 6. 1988, p. 32).

Article 2

The President of the Council shall, on behalf of the European Economic Community, deposit the instrument of approval with the Government of Portugal as provided for in Article 24 (2) of the Agreement.

Done at Luxembourg, 20 October 1993.

For the Council

The President

A. BOURGEOIS

COOPERATION AGREEMENT
for the protection of the coasts and waters of the north-east Atlantic against pollution

THE GOVERNMENT OF THE KINGDOM OF SPAIN,

THE GOVERNMENT OF THE FRENCH REPUBLIC,

THE GOVERNMENT OF THE KINGDOM OF MOROCCO,

THE GOVERNMENT OF THE PORTUGUESE REPUBLIC,

THE EUROPEAN ECONOMIC COMMUNITY,

meeting in the Conference for the protection of the coasts and waters of the north-east Atlantic against pollution due to hydrocarbons and other harmful substances, held in Lisbon on 17 October 1990,

AWARE of the need to protect the human environment in general and the marine environment in particular;

RECOGNIZING that pollution of the north-east Atlantic Ocean by hydrocarbons and other harmful substances may threaten the marine environment in general and the interests of coastal States in particular;

NOTING that such pollution has many origins, but RECOGNIZING that special measures are necessary in the event of accidents and other pollution incidents caused by ships and fixed and floating platforms ;

CONCERNED to act promptly and effectively in the event of a pollution incident at sea which would endanger the coasts or the related interests of a coastal State, with a view to reducing the damage caused by such an incident;

STRESSING the importance of genuine preparation at national level to combat pollution incidents at sea;

RECOGNIZING MOREOVER that it is important that reciprocal assistance and international cooperation be instituted amongst States in order to protect their coasts and their related interests;

EMPHASIZING also the importance of measures taken individually and jointly in order to minimize the risks of pollution incidents at sea;

MINDFUL of the success of current regional agreements, and in particular of the action plan of the European Communities, the aim of which is to provide aid in the event of major marine pollution by hydrocarbons or other dangerous substances,

have designated their Plenipotentiaries, who, having exchanged their full powers, found in good and due form,

HAVE AGREED AS FOLLOWS:

Article 1

The Contracting Parties to this Agreement (hereinafter referred to as 'the Parties') undertake, individually or jointly as the case may be, to take all appropriate measures under this Agreement in order to be prepared to deal with an incident of pollution at sea such as pollution caused by hydrocarbons or other harmful substances.

Article 2

For the purposes of this Agreement:

'*pollution incident*' means an event or series of events having the same origin and resulting in a discharge or a danger of a discharge of hydrocarbons or other harmful substances which has occasioned or may occasion damage to the marine environment, the coast or the related interests of one or more of the Parties, and requiring emergency action or an immediate reaction of some other kind;

'*hydrocarbons*' means oil in all its forms in particular crude oil, fuel oil, muds, hydrocarbon residues and other refined products;

'*other harmful substances*' means all substances other than hydrocarbons, including harzardous waste, the release of which into the marine environment may be harmful to human health, ecosystems or living resources, coasts or the related interests of the Parties.

Article 3

The geographical scope of this Agreement shall be the north-east Atlantic region bounded by the outer limit of the exclusive economic zones of each of the contracting States and:

a) to the north by a line drawn from east to west as follows: starting from the southernmost point of the island of Quessant (Ushant) and following the parallel 48° 27' N as far as its intersection with the south-west limit of the Agreement for cooperation in dealing with pollution of the North Sea by oil and other harmful substances (Bonn Agreement); thence following the south-west limit of the said Bonn Agreement as far as its intersection with the line marking the limit of the continental shelf between France and the United Kingdom of Great Britain and Northern Ireland defined by the arbitration decision of 30 June 1977; thence following the said line as far as its western extremity situated at point N with the coordinates 48° 06' 00'' N and 9° 36' 30'' W;

b) to the east by the western limit of the Convention for the protection of the Mediterranean Sea against pollution (Barcelona Convention) of 16 February 1976;

c) to the south by the southern limit of the waters covered by the sovereignty or jurisdiction of the Kingdom of Morocco.

Article 4

1.   'Each of the States' Parties to this Agreement shall set up within its territory, if necessary in collaboration with the industries concerned, including the shipping industry, and other bodies, and shall maintain in operational condition a minimum amount of equipment at predetermined points in order to be able to deal with discharges of hydrocarbons or other harmful substances.

2.   Each of the Parties shall set up a national system to prevent and combat incidents of pollution at sea. This system shall encompass:

a) a description of the administrative organization and of the responsibility of each of its components for the preparation and implementation of measures to prevent and combat pollution, and in particular of the national authority responsible for dealing with questions of mutual assistance with the other Parties;

b) the particulars of a national operational contact point to be responsible for receiving and issuing reports on pollution incidents at sea, as mentioned in Article 8 (3) of this Agreement;

c) a national plan of action to prevent or to deal with such pollution incidents. The said plan of action shall comprise, inter alia:

i) identifying likely sources of discharge of hydrocarbons or other
harmful substances;

ii) identifying endangered sensitive areas and vulnerable resources in
danger, and priorities for their protection;

iii) itemizing the equipment and human resources available;

iv) specifying the means for storing and disposing of the hydrocarbons
or other harmful substances recovered.

3. Furthermore, each of the Parties shall, individually or within the framework of bilateral or multilateral cooperation, set up staff training programmes
to improve the state of readiness of the bodies responsible for dealing with pollution.

Article 5

1. The Parties shall jointly draw up and determine guidelines covering the
practical, operational and technical aspects of joint action.

2. To facilitate active cooperation, each of the Parties shall undertake to
provide the other Parties with the information referred to in Article 4 (2) (a)
and (b), and information on:

a) its national resources (equipment and staff) intended for preventing and
dealing with such pollution, of which, at the time of a pollution incident, some could be made available within the framework of international assistance under conditions to be determined between the Parties
concerned;

b) new methods to avoid such pollution and effective new techniques for
dealing with it;

c) the main pollution incidents on which it has had to take action.

Article 6

The cooperation provided for in the preceding Articles shall also apply in the
event of loss at sea of harmful substances placed in packages, freight containers, portable containers or in lorry, trailer or rail tankers.

Article 7

1.   Each of the Parties shall require its officials with powers in this context, and captains and others responsible for vessels flying its flag or for marine platforms operated in areas falling within its jurisdiction, to report forthwith the occurrence of any incident on their vessels or platforms involving the discharge or danger of discharge of hydrocarbons or other harmful substances. In the case of vessels, these reports shall comply with the provisions drawn up by the Intergovernmental Maritime Consultative Organization.

2.   Each of the Parties shall issue instructions to the vessels and aircraft of its maritime inspectorate and other departments that they are to report, without delay, any incident of pollution due to hydrocarbons or other harmful substances which they have observed.

3.   Each of the Parties shall request the captains of all vessels flying its flag and the pilots of all aircraft registered in its territory to report without delay the presence, nature and extent of the hydrocarbons or other harmful substances observed which may constitute a danger for the coast or related interests of one or more of the Parties.

Article 8

1.   For the sole purposes of this Agreement, the north-east Atlantic region shall be divided into areas as defined in Annex 1 to this Agreement.

2.   A Party in whose area a pollution incident occurs shall conduct the requisite evaluations as to its nature, magnitude and possible consequences.

3.   Where the magnitude of the pollution incident so warrants, the Party concerned shall immediately inform all other Parties through their operational contact points of any action taken to combat the hydrocarbons or other harmful substances. It shall keep these substances under observation for as long as they are present in its area and shall keep the other Parties informed of developments concerning the pollution incident and of the measures taken or planned.

4.   When oil slicks or floating substances drift into an adjacent area, the responsibility for the evelution and for the notification of the other Parties, as stipulated above, shall be transferred to the Party in whose area the hydrocarbons or substances are now located, unless otherwise agreed by the Parties concerned.

Article 9

1.   The Parties may designate areas of joint interest.

2.   If pollution occurs in an area of joint interest, the Party in whose area of responsibility the incident occurs shall not merely inform the neighbouring Party immediately as required by Article 8 (3) but shall also invite that Party to take part in the evaluation of the nature of the incident and to decide whether the incident must be regarded as being of sufficient gravity and magnitude to warrant joint action by both Parties in combating it.

3.   Subject to the provisions of paragraph 4 of this Article, the responsibility for initiating such joint action shall lie with the Party in whose area of responsibility the incident occurs. This Party shall designate an authority and instruct it to coordinate action; the said authority shall then assume responsibility for action, request any aid which may be needed and coordinate all available resources. The neighbouring Party shall provide such appropriate support as its resources permit and shall likewise appoint an authority for the liaison of action.

4.   The neighbouring Party may assume responsibility for coordinating action subject to an agreement with the Party in whose area of responsibility the incident occurs where:

a) the neighbouring Party is directly threatened by the incident; or

b) the vessel or vessels in question flies or fly the flag of the neighbouring Party; or

c) the greater part of the resources likely to be used in the operation to combat pollution belong to the neighbouring Party.

If this paragraph is invoked, the Party in whose area of responsibility of incident occurs shall give the Party assuming responsibility for the coordination of action all requisite assistance.

Article 10

A Party requiring assistance to deal with pollution or a threat of pollution at sea or off its coast may request help from the other Parties. The Party requesting assistance shall specify the type of assistance which it requires, if need be by seeking the opinion of other Parties. Parties from whom help is requested under this Article shall make every endeavour to provide such help in so far as their resources permit, taking into consideration, particularly in the event of pollution by harmful substances other than hydrocarbons, the technical resources at their disposal.

Article 11

1.   No provision in this Agreement shall prejudice in any manner whatsoever the sovereignty of States over their territorial waters, or the jurisdiction and sovereign rights which they exercise in their exclusive economic zones and over the continental shelf pursuant to international law, or the exercise by vessels and aircraft of all States of the rights and freedom of navigation as governed by international law and in accordance with the relevant international instruments.

2.   Under no circumstances may the division into areas referred to in Articles 8 and 9 of this Agreement be invoked as a precedent or as an argument in respect of sovereignty or jurisdiction.

Article 12

Each of the Parties shall develop means for monitoring shipping by setting up departments dealing with shipping movements. The Parties shall, to that end, consult each other regularly and shall participate actively in the studies needed for such development within the competent international bodies, including studies into linking up national departments dealing with shipping movements.

Article 13

1.   In the absence of any bilateral or multilateral agreement which may be concluded on the financial provisions governing action taken by the Parties to combat pollution at sea, the Parties shall bear the costs of their respective action to combat such pollution in accordance with the principles stated below:

   a) if action is taken by one Party at the express request of another, the Party which had requested the help shall refund to the other Party the expenses entailed by its action;

   b) if action is taken solely upon the initiative of one Party, that Party shall bear the costs entailed by its action;

   c) if action is taken in an area of joint interest by the Parties concerned by that area, as defined in Article 9, each Party shall bear the costs entailed by its own action.

2.   The Party which requested assistance shall be free to terminate its request at any time but shall, in that case, bear the expenses already disbursed or incurred by the assisting Contracting Party.

3. Unless otherwise agreed, expenses entailed by action undertaken by one Party at the express request of another shall be calculated by a responsible person or body, where appropriate on the basis of an expert report, in accordance with the legislation and current practice of the assisting country for the reimbursement of such expenditure.

Article 14

1. Article 13 of this Agreement may not in any circumstances be interpreted as prejudicing the rights of the Parties to recover from third parties the costs involved in actions undertaken to deal with pollution or a threat of pollution pursuant to other provisions and rules applicable under national and international law.

2. The Parties may cooperate and provide mutual assistance in recovering the costs involved in their actions.

Article 15

1. Meetings of the Parties to this Agreement shall be held at regular intervals or at any time when, owing to special circumstances, it shall be decided to do so pursuant to the rules of procedure.

2. In the course of their first meetings, the Parties shall draw up rules of procedure and financial regulations, which shall be adopted by a unanimous vote.

3. The depositary government shall convene the first meeting of the Parties as soon as possible following entry into force of this Agreement.

Article 16

In the areas falling within its jurisdiction, the European Economic Community shall exercise its voting right with a number of votes equal to the number of its Member States which are Parties to this Agreement. The European Economic Community shall not exercise its voting right in cases where Member States exercise theirs and vice versa.

Article 17

Meetings of the Parties shall be responsible for:

a) general monitoring of implementation of this Agreement;

b) regular examination of the effectiveness of measures taken pursuant to this Agreement;

c) endeavouring as soon as possible to identify and define those areas which, owing to their environmental characteristics, must be regarded as particularly sensitive;

d) carrying out any other functions which may be necessary in accordance with the provisions of this Agreement.

Article 18

1. An International Centre shall be set up with the aim of assisting those States which are Parties to react swiftly and effectively to pollution incidents.

2. This Centre, having its seat in the depositary State, shall cooperate with existing bodies in the other Parties in order to ensure the desired swiftness and effectiveness throughout the region covered by this Agreement and, where necessary, outside that region.

3. The meeting of the Parties shall define the functions of the Centre on the basis of the guidelines given in Annex 2.

Article 19

1. The International Centre shall prepare suitable proposals for the Parties with the aim of improving the mobility and complementary nature of the material facilities of the various Parties.

2. Recommendations shall be aimed in particular at operations to renew or increase national stocks.

Article 20

1.   Without prejudice to the provisions of Annex 1.3 of this Agreement, any proposal from one of the Parties with a view to amendment of this Agreement or its Annexes shall be studied at a meeting of the Parties. Following adoption of the proposal by a unanimous vote, the Parties shall be notified of the amendment by the depositary government.

2.   Such an amendment shall enter into force on the first day of the second month following the date on which the depositary government receives notification of its approval by all Contracting Parties.

Article 21

1.   Each Contracting Party shall contribute 2,5 % of the expenditure involved in the secretariat function for this Agreement as referred to in Annex 2.7. Two-thirds of the balance of this expenditure shall be covered by the depositary government, and the remaining third by the other States as follows:

—   the Kingdom of Spain: 40 %,

—   the French Republic: 40 %,

—   the Kingdom of Morocco: 20 %.

2.   The other functions of the Centre which are referred to in Annex 2 shall be covered as far as possible by voluntary contributions from the Parties, the amount of which shall be indicated at the meeting of the Contracting Parties.

Article 22

1.   The signatory States and the European Economic Community become Parties to this Agreement either by signature without reservation as to ratification, acceptance or approval followed by ratification, acceptance or approval.

2.   The instruments of ratification, acceptance or approval shall be deposited with the Government of Portugal.

3.   This Agreement shall enter into force on the first day of the second month following the date on which all the States referred to in this Article and the European Economic Community sign without reservation as to ratification, acceptance or approval or deposit an instrument of ratification, acceptance or approval.

Article 23

1.   The Parties may unanimously invite any other State having a north-east Atlantic coast to accede to this Agreement.

2.   If they do so, Articles 3 and 21 of this Agreement and Annex 1 hereto shall be amended accordingly. Any amendments shall be adopted by a unanimous vote at a meeting of the Contracting Parties and shall take effect at the time of entry into force of this Agreement for the acceding State.

Article 24

1.   For each State acceding to this Agreement, the latter shall enter into force on the first day of the second month following the date on which the State concerned deposits its instrument of accession.

2.   Instruments of accession shall be deposited with the Government of Portugal.

Article 25

1.   After five years this Agreement may be denounced by any Party.

2.   Denunciation shall be effected by a notification in writing addressed to the depositary government, which shall notify all the other Parties of any denunciation received and of the date of its receipt.

3.   A denunciation shall take effect one year after its receipt by the depositary government.

Article 26

The depositary government shall inform those States which have signed this Agreement or acceded thereto, and the European Economic Community, of:

a)   any signing of this Agreement;

b)   the depositing of instruments of ratification, acceptance, approval or accession and the receipt of notice of denunciation;

c)   the date of entry into force of this Agreement;

d)   the receipt of notifications of approval concerning amendments made to this Agreement or its Annexes and the date of entry into force of those amendments.

Article 27

The original of this Agreement, drawn up in the Arabic, Spanish, French and Portuguese languages, the French text being authentic in case of divergence, shall be deposited with the Government of Portugal, which shall communicate certified copies to the Contracting Parties and which shall transmit a certified copy to the Secretary-General of the United Nations Organization for registration and publication, in application of Article 102 of the Charter of the United Nations.

In witness whereof, the undersigned Plenipotentiaries have hereunto set their hands and affixed their seals.

Done at Lisbon, 17 October 1990.

FOR THE GOVERNMENT OF THE FRENCH REPUBLIC

Minister for the Sea (Ministry of Infrastructure, Housing, Transport and the Sea),

Jacques Mellick.

FOR THE GOVERNMENT OF THE KINGDOM OF SPAIN,

Minister for Public Works and Town Planning,

Javier Sáenz Cosculluela.

FOR THE GOVERNMENT OF THE KINGDOM OF MOROCCO,

Minister for the Interior and for Information,

Driss Basri.

FOR THE GOVERNMENT OF THE PORTUGUESE REPUBLIC,

Minister for the Environment and Natural Resources,

Fernando Real.

FOR THE EUROPEAN ECONOMIC COMMUNITY,

Member of the Commission of the European Communities with special responsibility for environmental protection,

Carlo Ripa di Meana.

ANNEX 1

1.   Subject to bilateral agreements concluded between the contracting States, the areas provided for in Article 8 (1) of this Agreement shall correspond to the exclusive economic zones of each of the contracting States.

2.   Any bilateral agreements which may be concluded in accordance with the previous paragraph shall be communicated to the depositary government, which shall transmit them to the Contracting Parties. They shall enter into force for all Contracting Parties on the first day of the sixth month following such transmission, unless, within a period of three months following that transmission, one of the Contracting Parties raises an objection or asks for consultations on the matter.

3.   Two or more States which are Parties may alter the common limits of their zones as defined in this Annex. Any such alteration shall enter into force for all Parties on the first day of the sixth month following the date of its communication by the depositary government, unless, within a period of three months following that communication, one of the Parties raises an objection or asks for consultations on the matter.

ANNEX 2

Guidelines for defining the functions of the International Action Centre

1.   Establishing close working relationships with other national and international centres in the region covered by the Agreement and, where necessary, outside that region.

2.   On the basis of the above principle and using all existing powers in the region, coordinating national and regional action with regard to training, technical cooperation and expertise in cases of emergency.

3.   Collecting and disseminating information on pollution incidents (inventories, expert opinions, reports on incidents, technical progress for improving action plans, etc.).

4.   Preparing systems for transmitting information, in particular to be exchanged in cases of emergency.

5.   Place for exchanges of information on techniques for monitoring marine pollution.

6.   Role of the Centre in cases of emergency.

7.   Secretariat for this Agreement.

8.   Management of that part of the Portuguese stock which may be made available to other Parties in other States outside the region. Also, where appropriate, coordination of the management of other similar national stocks (in particular, this function could be envisaged in the case of additional stocks for which there has been a Community or international financial contribution).

DECISION 94/1/ECSC, EC[1] OF THE COUNCIL AND THE COMMISSION
of 13 December 1993
on the conclusion of the Agreement on the European Economic Area between the European Communities, their Member States and the Republic of Austria, the Republic of Finland, the Republic of Iceland, the Principality of Liechtenstein, the Kingdom of Norway, the Kingdom of Sweden and the Swiss Confederation

THE COUNCIL OF THE EUROPEAN UNION,

THE COMMISSION OF THE EUROPEAN COMMUNITIES,

Having regard to the Treaty establishing the European Coal and Steel Community,

Having regard to the Treaty establishing the European Community, and in particular Article 238 in conjunction with Article 228 (3), second subparagraph thereof,

Having regard to the assent of the European Parliament[2],

Whereas the Agreement on the European Economic Area between the European Communities, their Member States and the Republic of Austria, the Republic of Finland, the Republic of Iceland, the Principality of Liechtenstein, the Kingdom of Norway, the Kingdom of Sweden and the Swiss Confederation, signed in Oporto on 2 May 1992 should be approved,

HAVE DECIDED AS FOLLOWS:

Article 1

The Agreement on the European Economic Area between the European Communities, their Member States and the Republic of Austria, the Republic of Finland, the Republic of Iceland, the Principality of Liechtenstein, the Kingdom of Norway, the Kingdom of Sweden and the Swiss Confederation, the Protocols, the Annexes annexed thereto and the Declarations, the Agreed Minutes and exchanges of letters attached to the Final Act are hereby approved

---

[1] OJ No L 1, 3. 1. 1994.
[2] OJ No C 305, 23. 11. 1992, p. 66.

on behalf of the European Community and the European Coal and Steel Community.

The texts of the acts referred to in the first paragraph are attached to this Decision.

Article 2

The act of approval provided for in Article 129 of the Agreement shall be deposited by the President of the Council on behalf of the European Community and by the President of the Commission on behalf of the European Coal and Steel Community[1].

Done at Brussels, 13 December 1993.

For the Council   *For the Commission*

The President   *The President*

Ph. MAYSTADT   J. DELORS

---

[1]   See page 606 of this Official Journal. (OJ No L 1, 3. 1. 1994)

AGREEMENT ON THE EUROPEAN ECONOMIC AREA

CHAPTER 3   ENVIRONMENT

Article 73

1)   Action by the Contracting Parties relating to the environment shall have the following objectives:

    a)   to preserve, protect and improve the quality of the environment;

    b)   to contribute towards protecting human health;

    c)   to ensure a prudent and rational utilization of natural resources.

2.   Action by the Contracting Parties relating to the environment shall be based on the principles that preventive action should be taken, that environmental damage should as a priority be rectified at source, and that the polluter should pay. Environmental protection requirements shall be a component of the Contracting Parties' other policies.

Article 74

Annex XX contains the specific provisions on protective measures which shall apply pursuant to Article 73.

Article 75

The protective measures referred to in Article 74 shall not prevent any Contracting Party from maintaining or introducing more stringent protective measures compatible with this Agreement.

ANNEX XX

ENVIRONMENT

List provided for in Article 74

INTRODUCTION

When the acts referred to in this Annex contain notions or refer to procedures which are specific to the Community legal order, such as

- preambles;
- the addressees of the Community acts;
- references to territories or languages of the EC;
- references to rights and obligations of EC Member States, their public entities, undertakings or individuals in relation to each other; and
- references to information and notification procedures;

Protocol 1 on horizontal adaptations shall apply, unless otherwise provided for in this Annex.

SECTORAL ADAPTATION

For the purposes of this Annex and notwithstanding the provisions of Protocol 1, the term 'Member State(s)' contained in the acts referred to shall be understood to include, in addition to its meaning in the relevant EC acts, Austria, Finland, Iceland, Liechtenstein, Norway, Sweden and Switzerland.

ACTS REFERRED TO

I.   **General**

1)   **385 L 0337:** Council Directive 85/337/EEC of 27 June 1985 on the assessment of the effects of certain public and private projects on the environment (OJ No L 175, 5.7.1985, p. 40).

2)   **390 L 0313:** Council Directive 90/313/EEC of 7 June 1990 on freedom of access to information (OJ No L 158, 23.6.1990, p. 56).

II.   Water

3)   **375 L 0440:** Council Directive 75/440/EEC of 16 June 1975 concerning the quality required of surface water intended for the abstraction of drinking water in the Member States (OJ No L 194, 25.7.1975, p. 26), as amended by:

—   **379 L 0869:** Council Directive 79/869/EEC of 9 October 1979 (OJ No L 271, 29.10.1979, p. 44).

4)   **376 L 0464:** Council Directive 76/464/EEC of 4 May 1976 on pollution caused by certain dangerous substances discharged into the aquatic environment of the Community (OJ L 129, 18.5.1976, p. 23).

The provisions of the Directive shall, for the purposes of the Agreement, be read with the following adaptation:

Iceland shall put into effect the measures necessary for it to comply with the provisions of this Directive as from 1 January 1995.

5)   **379 L 0869:** Council Directive 79/869/EEC of 9 October 1979 concerning the methods of measurement and frequencies of sampling and analysis of surface water intended for the abstraction of drinking water in the Member States (OJ L 271, 29.10.1979, p. 44), as amended by:

—   **381 L 0855:** Council Directive 81/855/EEC of 19 October 1981 (OJ No L 319, 7.11.1981, p. 16),

—   **1 85 I:** Act concerning the Conditions of Accession and Adjustments to the Treaties — Accession to the European Communities of the Kingdom of Spain and the Portuguese Republic (OJ No L 302, 15.11.1985, p. 219).

6)   **380 L 0068:** Council Directive 80/68/EEC of 17 December 1979 on the protection of groundwater against pollution caused by certain dangerous substances (OJ No L 20, 26.1.1980, p. 43).

The provisions of the Directive shall, for the purposes of the Agreement, be read with the following adaptation:

the provisions of Article 14 shall not apply.

7)   **380 L 0778:** Council Directive 80/778/EEC of 15 July 1980 relating to the quality of water intended for human consumption (OJ No L 229, 30.8.1980, p. 11), as amended by:

—   **381 L 0858:** Council Directive 81/858/EEC of 19 October 1981 (OJ No L 319, 7.11.1981, p. 19).

—   **1 85 I:** Act concerning the Conditions of Accession and Adjustments to the Treaties — Accession to the European Communities of the

Kingdom of Spain and the Portuguese Republic
(OJ No L 302, 15.11.1985, pp. 219, 397).

The provisions of the Directive shall, for the purposes of the Agreement, be read with the following adaptation:

the provisions of Article 20 shall not apply.

8) **382 L 0176:** Council Directive 82/176/EEC of 22 March 1982 on limit values and quality objectives for mercury discharges by the chlor-alkali electrolysis industry (OJ No L 81, 27.3.1982, p. 29).

The provisions of the Directive shall, for the purposes of the present Agreement, be read with the following adaptation:

Iceland shall put into effect the measures necessary for it to comply with the provisions of this Directive as from 1 January 1995.

9) **383 L 0513:** Council Directive 83/513/EEC of 26 September 1983 on limit values and quality objectives for cadmium discharges (OJ No L 291, 24.10.1983, p. 1).

The provisions of the Directive shall, for the purposes of the Agreement, be read with the following adaptation:

Iceland shall put into effect the measures necessary for it to comply with the provisions of this Directive as from 1 January 1995.

10) **384 L 0156:** Council Directive 84/156/EEC of 8 March 1984 on limit values and quality objectives for mercury discharges by sectors other than the chlor-alkali electrolysis industry (OJ No L 74, 17.3.1984, p. 49).

The provisions of the Directive shall, for the purposes of the Agreement, be read with the following adaptation:

Iceland shall put into effect the measures necessary for it to comply with the provisions of this Directive as from 1 January 1995.

11) **384 L 0491**: Council Directive 84/491/EEC of 9 October 1984 on limit values and quality objectives for discharges of hexachlorocyclohexane (OJ No L 274, 17.10.1984, p. 11).

The provisions of the Directive shall, for the purposes of the Agreement, be read with the following adaptation:

Iceland shall put into effect the measures necessary for it to comply with the provisions of this Directive as from 1 January 1995.

12) **386 L 0280:** Council Directive 86/280/EEC of 12 June 1986 on limit values and quality objectives for discharges of certain dangerous substances included in List I of the Annex to Directive 76/464/EEC (OJ No L 181, 4.7.1986, p. 16), as amended by:

— **388 L 0347:** Council Directive 88/347/EEC of 16 June 1988 amending Annex II to Directive 86/280/EEC (OJ No L 158, 25.6.1988, p. 35),

— **390 L 0415:** Council Directive 90/415/EEC of 27 July 1990 amending Annex II to Directive 86/280/EEC (OJ No L 219, 14.8.1990, p. 49).

The provisions of the Directive shall, for the purposes of the Agreement, be read with the following adaptation:

Iceland shall put into effect the measures necessary for it to comply with the provisions of this Directive as from 1 January 1995.

13) **391 L 0271:** Council Directive 91/271/EEC of 21 May 1991 concerning urban waste water treatment (OJ No L 135, 30.5.1991, p. 40).

The provisions of the Directive shall, for the purposes of the Agreement, be read with the following adaptation:

Iceland shall put into effect the measures necessary for it to comply with the provisions of this Directive as from 1 January 1995.

III. Air

14) **380 L 0779:** Council Directive 80/779/EEC of 15 July 1980 on air quality limit values and guide values for sulphur dioxide and suspended particulates (OJ No L 229, 30.8.1980, p. 30), as amended by:

— **381 L 0857:** Council Directive 81/857/EEC of 19 October 1981 (OJ No L 319, 7.11.1981, p. 18),

— **1 85 I:** Act concerning the Conditions of Accession and Adjustments to the Treaties — Accession to the European Communities of the Kingdom of Spain and the Portuguese Republic (OJ No L 302, 15.11.1985, p. 219),

— **389 L 0427:** Council Directive 89/427/EEC of 21 June 1989 (OJ No L 201, 14.7.1989, p. 53).

The provisions of the Directive shall, for the purposes of the Agreement, be read with the following adaptation:

Iceland shall put into effect the measures necessary for it to comply with the provisions of this Directive as from 1 January 1995.

15) **382 L 0884:** Council Directive 82/884/EEC of 3 December 1982 on a limit value for lead in the air (OJ No L 378, 31.12.1982, p. 15).

The provisions of the Directive shall, for the purposes of the Agreement, be read with the following adaptation:

Iceland shall put into effect the measures necessary for it to comply with the provisions of this Directive as from 1 January 1995.

16) **384 L 0360:** Council Directive 84/360/EEC of 28 June 1984 on the combating of air pollution from industrial plants (OJ No L 188, 16.7.1984, p. 20).

The provisions of the Directive shall, for the purposes of the Agreement, be read with the following adaptation:

Iceland shall put into effect the measures necessary for it to comply with the provisions of this Directive as from 1 January 1995.

17) **385 L 0203:** Council Directive 85/203/EEC of 7 March 1985 on air-quality standards for nitrogen dioxide (OJ No L 87, 27.3.1985, p. 1), as amended by:

— **385 L 0580:** Council Directive 85/580/EEC of 20 December 1985 (OJ No L 372, 31.12.1985, p. 36).

The provisions of the Directive shall, for the purposes of the Agreement, be read with the following adaptation:

Iceland shall put into effect the measures necessary for it to comply with the provisions of this Directive as from 1 January 1995.

18) **387 L 0217:** Council Directive 87/217/EEC of 19 March 1987 on the prevention and reduction of environmental pollution by asbestos (OJ No L 85, 28.3.1987, p. 40).

The provisions of the Directive shall, for the purposes of the Agreement, be read with the following adaptations:

a) in Article 9 'the Treaty' shall read 'the EEA Agreement';

b) Iceland shall put into effect the measures necessary for it to comply with the provisions of this Directive as from 1 January 1995.

19) **388 L 0609:** Council Directive 88/609/EEC of 24 November 1988 on the limitation of emissions of certain pollutants into the air from large combustion plants (OJ No L 336, 7.12.1988, p. 1).

The provisions of the Directive shall, for the purposes of the Agreement, be read with the following adaptations:

a) Article 3(5) shall be replaced by the following:

' 5 (a) If a substantial and unexpected change in energy demand or in the availability of certain fuels or certain generating installations creates serious technical difficulties for the implementation by a Contracting Party of the emission ceilings, such a Contracting Party may request a modification of the emission ceilings and/or dates set out in Annexes I and II. The procedure set out in (b) shall apply.

(b) The Contracting Party shall immediately inform the other Contracting Parties through the EEA Joint Committee of such action and give reasons for its decision. If a Contracting Party so requires, consultations on the appropriateness of the measures taken shall take place in the EEA Joint Committee. Part VII of the Agreement shall apply.';

b) the following shall be added to the table for ceilings and reduction targets in Annex I:

	0	1	2	3	4	5	6	7	8	9
Austria	171	102	68	51	-40	-60	-70	-40	-60	-70
Finland	90	54	36	27	-40	-60	-70	-40	-60	-70
Sweden	112	67	45	34	-40	-60	-70	-40	60	-70
Switzerland	28	14	14	14	-50	-50	-50	-50	-50	-50

';

c) the following is added to the table for ceilings and reduction targets in Annex II:

	0	1	2	3	4	5	6
Austria	81	65	48	-20	-40	-20	-40
Finland	19	15	11	-20	-40	-20	-40
Sweden	31	25	19	-20	-40	-20	-40
Switzerland	9	8	5	-10	-40	-10	-40

';

d) at the time of entry into force of the Agreement, Iceland, Liechtenstein and Norway do not have any large combustion plants as defined in Article 1. These States will comply with the Directive if and when they acquire such plants.

20) **389 L 0369:** Council Directive 89/369/EEC of 8 June 1989 on the prevention of air pollution from new municipal waste-incineration plants (OJ No L 163, 14.6.1989, p. 32).

The provisions of the Directive shall, for the purposes of the Agreement, be read with the following adaptation:

Iceland shall put into effect the measures necessary for it to comply with the provisions of this Directive as from 1 January 1995.

21) **389 L 0429:** Council Directive 89/429/EEC of 21 June 1989 on the reduction of air pollution from existing municipal waste-incineration plants (OJ No L 203, 15.7.1989, p. 50).

IV. **Chemicals, industrial risk and biotechnology**

22) **376 L 0403:** Council Directive 76/403/EEC of 6 April 1976 on the disposal of polychlorinated biphenyls and polychlorinated terphenyls (OJ No L 108, 26.4.1976, p. 41).

The provisions of the Directive shall, for the purposes of the Agreement, be read with the following adaptation:

The EFTA States shall put into effect the measures necessary for them to comply with the provisions of this Directive as from 1 January 1995, subject to a review before that date.

23) **382 L 0501:** Council Directive 82/501/EEC of 24 June 1982 on the major accident hazards of certain industrial activities
(OJ No L 230, 5.8.1982, p. 1), as amended by:

— **1 85 I:** Act concerning the Conditions of Accession and Adjustments to the Treaties — Accession to the European Communities of the Kingdom of Spain and the Portuguese Republic
(OJ No L 302, 15.11.1985, p. 219),

— **387 L 0216:** Council Directive 87/216/EEC of 19 March 1987
(OJ No L 85, 28.3.1987, p. 36),

— **388 L 0610**: Council Directive 88/610/EEC of 24 November 1988
(OJ No L 336, 7.12.1988, p. 14).

24) **390 L 0219:** Council Directive 90/219/EEC of 23 April 1990 on the contained use of genetically modified micro-organisms
(OJ No L 117, 8.5.1990, p. 1).

The provisions of the Directive shall, for the purposes of the Agreement, be read with the following adaptation:

Austria, Finland, Iceland, Liechtenstein, Norway and Sweden shall put into effect the measures necessary for them to comply with the provisions of this Directive as from 1 January 1995.

25) **390 L 0220:** Council Directive 90/220/EEC of 23 April 1990 on the deliberate release into the environment of genetically modified organisms (OJ No L 117, 8.5.1990, p. 15).

The provisions of the Directive shall, for the purposes of the present Agreement, be read with the following adaptations:

a) Austria, Finland, Iceland, Liechtenstein, Norway and Sweden shall put into effect the measures necessary for them to comply with the provisions of this Directive as from 1 January 1995;

b) Article 16 shall be replaced by the following:

' 1. Where a Contracting Party has justifiable reasons to consider that a product which has been properly notified and has received written consent under this Directive constitutes a risk to human health or the environment, it may restrict or prohibit the use and/or sale of that product on its territory. It shall immediately inform the other Contracting Parties through the EEA Joint Committee of such action and give reasons for its decision.

2. If a Contracting Party so requires, consultations on the appropriateness of the measures taken shall take place in the EEA Joint Committee. Part VII of the Agreement shall apply.';

c) The Contracting Parties agree that the Directive only covers aspects relating to the potential risks to humans, plants, animals and the environment.

The EFTA States therefore reserve the right to apply their national legislation in this area in relation to other concerns than health and environment, in so far as it is compatible with this Agreement.

V. Waste

26) **375 L 0439:** Council Directive 75/439/EEC of 16 June 1975 on the disposal of waste oils (OJ No L 194, 25.7.1975, p. 23), as amended by:

— **387 L 0101:** Council Directive 87/101/EEC of 22 December 1986 (OJ No L 42, 12.2.1987, p. 43).

27) **375 L 0442:** Council Directive 75/442/EEC of 15 July 1975 on waste (OJ No L 194, 25.7.1975, p. 39), as amended by:

— **391 L 0156:** Council Directive 91/156/EEC of 18 March 1991 (OJ No L 78, 26.3.1991, p. 32).

The provisions of the Directive shall, for the purposes of the Agreement, be read with the following adaptation:

Norway shall put into effect the measures necessary for it to comply with the provisions of this Directive as from 1 January 1995, subject to a review before that date.

28) **378 L 0176:** Council Directive 78/176/EEC of 20 February 1978 on waste from the titanium-dioxide industry (OJ No L 54, 25.2.1978, p. 19), as amended by:

— **382 L 0883:** Council Directive 82/883/EEC of 3 December 1982 on procedures for the surveillance and monitoring of environments concerned by waste from the titanium-dioxide industry (OJ No L 378, 31.12.1982, p. 1),

— **383 L 0029:** Council Directive 83/29/EEC of 24 January 1983 (OJ No L 32, 3.2.1983, p. 28).

29) **378 L 0319:** Council Directive 78/319/EEC of 20 March 1978 on toxic and dangerous waste (OJ No L 84, 31.3.1978, p. 43), as amended by:

— **1 79 H:** Act concerning the Conditions of Accession and Adjustments to the Treaties — Accession to the European Communities of the Hellenic Republic (OJ No L 291, 19.11.1979, p. 111),

— **1 85 I:** Act concerning the Conditions of Accession and Adjustments to the Treaties — Accession to the European Communities of the Kingdom of Spain and the Portuguese Republic (OJ No L 302, 15.11.1985, pp. 219, 397).

The provisions of the Directive shall, for the purposes of the Agreement, be read with the following adaptation:

the EFTA States shall put into effect the measures necessary for them to comply with the provisions of this Directive as from 1 January 1995, subject to a review before that date.

30) **382 L 0883:** Council Directive 82/883/EEC of 3 December 1982 on procedures for the surveillance and monitoring of environments concerned by waste from the titanium-dioxide industry (OJ No L 378, 31.12.1982, p. 1), as amended by:

— **1 85 I:** Act concerning the Conditions of Accession and Adjustments to the Treaties — Accession to the European Communities of the Kingdom of Spain and the Portuguese Republic (OJ No L 302, 15.11.1985, p. 219).

31) **384 L 0631:** Council Directive 84/631/EEC of 6 December 1984 on the supervision and control within the European Community of the transfrontier shipment of hazardous waste (OJ No L 326, 13.12.1984, p. 31), as amended by:

— **385 L 0469:** Commission Directive 85/469/EEC of 22 July 1985 (OJ No L 272, 12.10.1985, p. 1),

— **386 L 0121:** Council Directive 86/121/EEC of 8 April 1986 (OJ No L 100, 16.4.1986, p. 20),

— **386 L 0279:** Council Directive 86/279/EEC of 12 June 1986 (OJ No L 181, 4.7.1986, p. 13).

The provisions of the Directive shall, for the purposes of the Agreement, be read with the following adaptations:

the following shall be added to box 36 of Annex I:

ÍSLENSKA	duft	duftkennt	fast	lúmkennt	seigfl-jótandi	bunnfl-jótandi	vökvi	loftkennt
NORSK	pulver-formet	stov-formet	fast	pasta-formet	viskost (tyktfly-tende)	slam-formet	flytende	gass-formet
SUOMESKI	jauhe-mäinen	pöly-mäinen	kiinteä	tahna-mäinen	siirappi-mäinen	liete-mäinen	neste-mäinen	kaasu-mäinen
SVENSKA	pulver-formigt	stoft	fast	pastöst	visköst	slamfor-migt	flytande	gasfor-migt

•unnfljótandi

støvformetviskøstl

                                                                          ';

d) the following new entries shall be added to the last sentence of provision 6 of Annex III: 'AU for Austria, SF for Finland, IS for Iceland, LI for Liechtenstein, NO for Norway, SE for Sweden and CH for Switzerland.';

e) the EFTA States shall put into effect the measures necessary for them to comply with the provisions of this Directive as from 1 January 1995, subject to a review before that date.

32) **386 L 0278:** Council Directive 86/278/EEC of 12 June 1986 on the protection of the environment, and in particular of the soil, when sewage sludge is used in agriculture (OJ No L 181, 4.7.1986, p. 6).

ACTS OF WHICH THE CONTRACTING PARTIES SHALL TAKE NOTE

The Contracting Parties take note of the content of the following acts:

33) **375 X 0436:** Council Recommendation 75/436/Euratom, ECSC, EEC of 3 March 1975 regarding cost allocation by public authorities on environmental matters (OJ No L 194, 25.7.1975, p. 1).

34) **379 X 0003:** Council Recommendation 79/3/EEC of 19 December 1978 to the Member States regarding methods of evaluating the cost of pollution control to industry (OJ No L 5, 9.1.1979, p. 28).

35) **380 Y 0830(01):** Council Resolution of 15 July 1980 on transboundary air pollution by sulphur dioxide and suspended particulates'
(OJ No C 222, 30.8.1980, p. 1).

36) **389 Y 1026(01):** Council Resolution (89/C 273/01) of 16 October 1989 on guidelines to reduce technological and natural hazards
(OJ No C 273, 26.10.1989, p. 1).

37) **390 Y 0518(01):** Council Resolution (90/C 122/02) of 7 May 1990 on waste policy (OJ No C 122, 18.5.1990, p. 2).

38) **SEC (89) 934 final:** Communication from the Commission to the Council and to Parliament of 18 September 1989. 'A Community strategy for waste management'.

COUNCIL DECISION 94/156/EC[1]
of 21 February 1994
on the accession of the Community to the Convention on the Protection of the Marine Environment of the Baltic Sea Area 1974 (Helsinki Convention)

THE COUNCIL OF THE EUROPEAN UNION,

Having regard to the Treaty establishing the European Community, and in particular Article 130s in conjunction with Article 228 (3), first subparagraph, thereof,

Having regard to the proposal from the Commission[2],

Having regard to the opinion of the European Parliament[3],

Having regard to the opinion of the Economic and Social Committee[4],

Whereas, according to Article 130r of the Treaty, Community policy on the environment is to contribute to the following objectives: preserving, protecting and improving the quality of the environment, protecting human health and the prudent and rational utilization of natural resources; whereas, furthermore, the Community and the Member States are cooperating, within the framework of their respective jurisdictions, with third countries and the relevant international organizations;

Whereas the Community has adopted measures in the area covered by the Convention on the Protection of the Marine Environment of the Baltic Sea Area 1974 (Helsinki Convention) and should act at international level in that area;

Whereas the Commission has been participating as an observer in the meetings of the Baltic Marine Environment Protection Commission since 19 February 1991;

Whereas the Commission has also been participating in the meetings of the ad hoc group set up to revise the Convention on the Protection of the Marine Environment of the Baltic Sea Area;

---

[1] OJ No L 73, 16. 3. 1994, p. 1.
[2] OJ No C 222, 18. 8. 1993, p. 13.
[3] OJ No C 315, 22. 11. 1993.
[4] OJ No C 34, 2. 2. 1994, p. 5.

103

Whereas the Convention on the Protection of the Marine Environment of the Baltic Sea Area has been the subject of amendments intended to permit the accession of the Community,

HAS DECIDED AS FOLLOWS:

Article 1

The European Community shall accede to the Convention on the Protection of the Marine Environment of the Baltic Sea Area 1974 (Helsinki Convention).

The text of the Convention is attached to this Decision.

Article 2

The President of the Council shall be authorized to designate the person or persons empowered to deposit the instrument of accession in accordance with Article 26 of the Convention.

Done at Brussels, 21 February 1994.

For the Council

The President

Th. PANGALOS

CONVENTION
on the Protection of the Marine Environment of the Baltic Sea Area, 1974 (Helsinki Convention)

THE STATES PARTIES TO THIS CONVENTION,

CONSCIOUS of the indispensable economic, social and cultural values of the marine environment of the Baltic Sea area and its living resources for the peoples of the Contracting Parties,

BEARING in mind the exceptional hydrographic and ecological characteristics of the Baltic Sea area and the sensitivity of its living resources to changes in the environment,

NOTING the rapid development of human activities at the Baltic Sea area, the considerable population living within its catchment area and the highly urbanized and industrialized state of the Contracting Parties as well as their intensive agriculture and forestry,

NOTING with deep concern the increasing pollution of the Baltic Sea area, originating from many sources such as discharges through rivers, estuaries, outfalls and pipelines, dumping and normal operations of vessels as well as through airborne pollutants,

CONSCIOUS of the responsibility of the Contracting Parties to protect and enhance the values of the marine environment of the Baltic Sea area for the benefit of their peoples,

RECOGNIZING that the protection and enhancement of the marine environment of the Baltic Sea area are tasks that cannot effectively be accomplished by national efforts only but that also close regional cooperation and other appropriate international measures aiming at fulfilling these tasks are urgently needed,

NOTING that the relevant recent international conventions even after having entered into force for the respective Contracting Parties do not cover all special requirements to protect and enhance the marine environment of the Baltic Sea area,

NOTING the importance of scientific and technological cooperation in the protection and enhancement of the marine environment of the Baltic Sea area, particularly between the Contracting Parties,

DESIRING to develop further regional cooperation in the Baltic Sea area, the possibilities and requirements of which were confirmed by the signing of the Convention on fishing and conservation of the living resources in the Baltic Sea and the Belts, Gdansk 1973,

CONSCIOUS of the importance or regional intergovernmental cooperation in the protection of the marine environment of the Baltic Sea area as an integral part of the peaceful cooperation and mutual understanding between all European States,

HAVE AGREED as follows:

Article 1   Convention area

For the purposes of the present Convention 'the Baltic Sea area' shall be the Baltic Sea proper with the Gulf of Bothnia, the Gulf of Finland and the entrance to the Baltic Sea bounded by the parallel of the Skaw in the Skagerrak at 5° 44' N. It does not include internal waters of the Contracting Parties.

Article 2   Definitions

For the purposes of the present Convention:

1) 'pollution' means introduction by man, directly or indirectly, of substances or energy into the marine environment, including estuaries, resulting in such deleterious effects as hazard to human health, harm to living resources and marine life, hindrance to legitimate uses of the sea including fishing, impairment of the quality for use of sea water, and reduction of amenities;

2) 'land-based pollution' means pollution of the sea caused by discharges from land reaching the sea waterborne, airborne or directly from the coast, including outfalls from pipelines;

3) a) 'dumping' means:

   i) any deliberate disposal at sea of wastes or other matter from vessels, aircraft, platforms or other man-made structures at sea;

   ii) any deliberate disposal at sea of vessels, aircraft, platforms or other man-made structures at sea;

   b) 'dumping' does not include:

   i) the disposal at sea of wastes or other matter incidental to, or derived from the normal operations of vessels, aircraft, platforms or other man-made structures at sea and their equipment, other than wastes or other matter transported by or to vessels, aircraft, platforms or other man-made structures at sea, operating for the purpose of disposal of such matter or derived from the treatment of such wastes or other matter on such vessels, aircraft, platforms or structures;

ii) placement of matter for a purpose other than the mere disposal thereof, provided that such placement is not contrary to the aims of the present Convention;

4) 'vessels and aircraft' means waterborne or airborne craft of any type whatsoever. This expression includes hydrofoil boats, air-cushion vehicles, submersibles, floating craft whether self-propelled or not, and fixed or floating platforms;

5) 'oil' means petroleum in any form including crude oil, fuel oil, sludge, oil refuse and refined products;

6) 'harmful substance' means any hazardous, noxious or other substance, which, if introduced into the sea, is liable to cause pollution;

7) 'incident' means an event involving the actual or probable discharge into the sea of a harmful substance, or effluents containing such a substance.

Article 3 Fundamental principles and obligations

1. The Contracting Parties shall individually or jointly take all appropriate legislative, administrative or other relevant measures in order to prevent and abate pollution and to protect and enhance the marine environment of the Baltic Sea area.

2. The Contracting Parties shall use their best endeavours to ensure that the implementation of the present Convention shall not cause an increase in the pollution of sea areas outside the Baltic Sea area.

Article 4 Application

1. The present Convention shall apply to the protection of the marine environment of the Baltic Sea area which comprises the water body and the sea bed including their living resources and other forms of marine life.

2. Without prejudice to the sovereign rights in regard to their territorial sea, each Contracting Party shall implement the provisions of the present Convention within its territorial sea through its national authorities.

3.   While the provisions of the present Convention do not apply to internal waters, which are under the sovereignty of each Contracting Party, the Contracting Parties undertake, without prejudice to the sovereign rights, to ensure that the purposes of the present Convention will be obtained in these waters.

4.   The present Convention shall not apply to any warship, naval auxiliary, military aircraft or other ship and aircraft owned or operated by a State and used, for the time being, only on government non-commercial service.

However, each Contracting Party shall ensure, by the adoption of appropriate measures not impairing the operations or operational capabilities of such ships and aircraft owned or operated by it, that such ships and aircraft act in a manner consistent, so far as is reasonable and practicable, with the present Convention.

Article 5   *Hazardous substances*

The Contracting Parties undertake to counteract the introduction, whether airborne, waterborne or otherwise, into the Baltic Sea area of hazardous substances as specified in Annex I to the present Convention.

Article 6   *Principles and obligations concerning land-based pollution*

1.   The Contracting Parties shall take all appropriate measures to control and minimize land-based pollution of the marine environment of the Baltic Sea area.

2.   In particular, the Contracting Parties shall take all appropriate measures to control and strictly limit pollution by noxious substances and materials in accordance with Annex II of the present Convention. To this end they shall, inter alia, as appropriate cooperate in the development and adoption of specific programmes, guidelines, standards or regulations concerning discharges, environmental quality, and products containing such substances and materials and their use.

3.   The substances and materials listed in Annex II of the present Convention shall not be introduced into the marine environment of the Baltic Sea area in significant quantities without a prior special permit, which may be periodically reviewed, by the appropriate national authority.

4.   The appropriate national authority will inform the commission referred to in Article 12 of the present Convention of the quantity, quality and way of discharge if it considers that significant quantities of substances and materials listed in Annex II of the present Convention were discharged.

5.   The Contracting Parties shall endeavour to establish and adopt common criteria for issuing permits for discharges.

6.   To control and minimize pollution of the Baltic Sea area by harmful substances the Contracting Parties shall, in addition to the provisions of Article 5 of the present Convention, aim at attaining the goals and applying the criteria enumerated in Annex III to the present Convention.

7.   If the discharge from a watercourse, flowing through the territories of two or more Contracting Parties or forming a boundary between them, is liable to cause pollution of the marine environment of the Baltic Sea area, the Contracting Parties concerned shall in common take appropriate measures in order to prevent and abate such pollution.

8.   The Contracting Parties shall endeavour to use best practicable means in order to minimize the airborne pollution of the Baltic Sea area by noxious substances.

Article 7   *Prevention of pollution from ships*

1.   In order to protect the Baltic Sea area from pollution by deliberate, negligent or accidental release of oil, harmful substances other than oil, and by the discharge of sewage and garbage from ships, the Contracting Parties shall take measures as set out in Annex IV to the present Convention.

2.   The Contracting Parties shall develop and apply uniform requirements for the capacity and location of facilities for the reception of residues of oil, harmful substances other than oil, including sewage and garbage, taking into account inter alia the special needs of passenger ships and combination carriers.

Article 8   *Pleasure craft*

The Contracting Parties shall, in addition to implementing those provisions of the present Convention which can appropriately be applied to pleasure craft, take special measures in order to abate harmful effects on the marine environment of the Baltic Sea area of pleasure craft activities. The measures shall inter alia deal with adequate reception facilities for wastes from pleasure craft.

Article 9   *Prevention of dumping*

1.   The Contracting Parties shall, subject to paragraphs 2 and 4 of this Article, prohibit dumping in the Baltic Sea area.

2.   Dumping of dredged spoils shall be subject to a prior special permit by the appropriate national authority in accordance with the provisions of Annex V to the present Convention.

3.   Each Contracting Party undertakes to ensure compliance with the provisions of this Article by vessels and aircraft:

a) registered in its territory or flying its flag;

b) loading, within its territory or territorial sea, matter which is to be dumped; or

c) believed to be engaged in dumping within its territorial sea.

4.   The provisions of this Article shall not apply when the safety of human life or of a vessel or aircraft at sea is threatened by the complete destruction or total loss of the vessel or aircraft, or in any case which constitutes a danger to human life, if dumping appears to be the only way of averting the threat and if there is every probability that the damage consequent upon such dumping will be less than would otherwise occur. Such dumping shall be so conducted as to minimize the likelihood of damage to human or marine life.

5.   Dumping made under the provisions of paragraph 4 of this Article shall be reported and dealt with in accordance with Annex VI to the present Convention and shall be reported forthwith to the commission referred to in Article 12 of the present Convention in accordance with the provisions of Regulation 4 of Annex V of the present Convention.

6.   In case of dumping suspected to be in contravention of the provisions of this Article the Contracting Parties shall cooperate in investigating the matter in accordance with Regulation 2 of Annex IV to the present Convention.

Article 10   Exploration and exploitation of the sea bed and its subsoil

Each Contracting Party shall take all appropriate measures in order to prevent pollution of the marine environment of the Baltic Sea area resulting from exploration or exploitation of its part of the sea bed and its subsoil or from any associated activities thereon. It shall also ensure that adequate equipment is at hand to start an immediate abatement of pollution in that area.

Article 11   *Cooperation in combating marine pollution*

The Contracting Parties shall take measures and cooperate as set out in Annex VI to the present Convention in order to eliminate or minimize pollution of the Baltic Sea area by oil or other harmful substances.

Article 12   *Institutional and organizational framework*

1.   The Baltic Marine Environment Protection Commission, hereinafter referred to as 'the Commission', is hereby established for the purposes of the present Convention.

2.   The chairmanship of the Commission shall be given to each Contracting Party in turn in alphabetical order of the names of the States in the English language.

The chairman shall serve for a period of two years, and cannot during the period of his chairmanship serve as representative of his country.

Should the chairmanship fall vacant, the Contracting Party chairing the Commission shall nominate a successor to remain in office until the term of chairmanship of that Contracting Party expires.

3.   Meetings of the Commission shall be held at least once a year upon convocation by the chairman. Upon the request of a Contracting Party, provided it is endorsed by another Contracting Party, the chairman shall, as soon as possible, summon an extraordinary meeting at such time and place as the chairman determines, however, not later than 90 days from the date of the submission of the request.

4.   The first meeting of the Commission shall be called by the depositary government and shall take place within a period of 90 days from the date following the entry into force of the present Convention.

5.   Each Contracting Party shall have one vote in the Commission. Unless otherwise provided under the present Convention, the Commission shall take its decisions unanimously.

Article 13   *The duties of the Commission*

The duties of the Commission shall be:

    a)   to keep the implementation of the present Convention under continuous observation;

b) to make recommendations on measures relating to the purposes of the present Convention;

c) to keep under review the contents of the present Convention including its Annexes and to recommend to the Contracting Parties such amendments to the present Convention including its Annexes as may be required including changes in the lists of substances and materials as well as the adoption of new Annexes;

d) to define pollution control criteria, objectives for the reduction of pollution, and objectives concerning measures, particularly according to Annex III of the present Convention;

e) to promote in close cooperation with appropriate governmental bodies, taking into consideration subparagraph (f) of this Article, additional measures to protect the marine environment of the Baltic Sea area and for this purpose:

i) to receive, process, summarize and disseminate from available sources relevant scientific, technological and statistical information; and

ii) to promote scientific and technological research;

f) to seek, when appropriate, the services of competent regional and other international organizations to collaborate in scientific and technological research as well as other relevant activities pertinent to the objectives of the present Convention;

g) to assume such other functions as may be appropriate under the terms of the present Convention.

Article 14   Administrative provisions for the Commission

1. The working language of the Commission shall be English.

2. The Commission shall adopt its rules of procedure.

3. The office of the Commission, hereafter referred to as the 'secretariat', shall be in Helsinki.

4. The Commission shall appoint an executive secretary and make provisions for the appointment of such other personnel as may be necessary, and determine the duties, terms and conditions of the executive secretary.

5. The executive secretary shall be the chief administrative official of the Commission and shall perform the functions that are necessary for the administration of the present Convention, the work of the Commission and other

tasks entrusted to the executive secretary by the Commission and its rules of procedure.

Article 15   *Financial provisions for the Commission*

1.   The Commission shall adopt its financial rules.

2.   The Commission shall adopt an annual or biennial budget of proposed expenditures and budget estimates for the fiscal period following thereafter. -

3.   The total amount of the budget, including any supplementary budget adopted by the Commission, shall be contributed by the Contracting Parties in equal parts, unless the Commission unanimously decides otherwise.

In addition to the contributions made by its Member States the European Economic Community will contribute at almost 2,5 % of the administrative costs of the budget.

4.   Each Contracting Party shall pay the expenses related to the participation in the Commission of its representatives, experts and advisers.

Article 16   *Scientific and technological cooperation*

1.   The Contracting Parties undertake directly, or when appropriate through competent regional or other international organizations, to cooperate in the fields of science, technology and other research, and to exchange data as well as other scientific information for the purposes of the present Convention.

2.   Without prejudice to paragraphs 1, 2 and 3 of Article 4 of the present Convention the Contracting Parties undertake directly, or when appropriate through competent regional or other international organizations, to promote studies, undertake, support or contribute to programmes aimed at developing ways and means for the assessment of the nature and extent of pollution, pathways, exposures, risks and remedies in the Baltic Sea area, and particularly to develop alternative methods of treatment, disposal and elimination of such matter and substances that are likely to cause pollution of the marine environment of the Baltic Sea area.

3.   The Contracting Parties undertake directly, or when appropriate through competent regional or other international organizations, and, on the basis of the information and data acquired pursuant to paragraphs 1 and 2 of this Article, to cooperate in developing inter-comparable observation

methods, in performing baseline studies and in establishing complementary or joint programmes for monitoring.

4. The organization and scope of work connected with the implementation of tasks referred to in the preceding paragraphs should primarily be outlined by the Commission.

Article 17 Responsibility for damage

The Contracting Parties undertake, as soon as possible, jointly to develop and accept rules concerning responsibility for damage resulting from acts or ommissions in contravention of the present Convention, including, inter alia, limits of responsibility, criteria and procedures for the determination of liability and available remedies.

Article 18 Settlement of disputes

1. In case of a dispute between Contracting Parties as to the interpretation or application of the present Convention, they should seek a solution by negotiation. If the Parties concerned cannot reach agreement they should seek the good offices of or jointly request the mediation by a third Contracting Party, a qualified international organization or a qualified person.

2. If the Parties concerned have not been able to resolve their dispute through negotiation or have been unable to agree on measures as described above, such disputes shall be, upon common agreement, submitted to an ad hoc arbitration tribunal, to a permanent arbitration tribunal, or to the International Court of Justice.

Article 19 Safeguard of certain freedoms

Nothing in the present Convention shall be construed as infringing upon the freedom of navigation, fishing, marine scientific research and other legitimate uses of the high seas, as well as upon the right of innocent passage through the territorial sea.

Article 20 Status of Annexes

The Annexes attached to the present Convention form an integral part of the Convention.

Article 21   Relation to other conventions

The provisions of the present Convention shall be without prejudice to the rights and obligations of the Contracting Parties under treaties concluded previously as well as under treaties which may be concluded in the future, furthering and developing the general principles of the law of the sea that the present Convention is based upon and in particular provisions concerning the prevention of pollution of the marine environment.

Article 22   Revision of the Convention

A conference for the purpose of a general revision of the present Convention may be convened with the consent of the Contracting Parties or at the request of the Commission.

Article 23   Amendments to the Articles of the Convention

1.   Each Contracting Party may propose amendments to the Articles of the present Convention. Any such proposed amendment shall be submitted to the depositary government and communicated by it to all Contracting Parties, which shall inform the depositary government of either their acceptance or rejection of the amendment as soon as possible after the receipt of the communication.

The amendment shall enter into force 90 days after the depositary government has received notifications of acceptance of that amendment from all Contracting Parties.

2.   With the consent of the Contracting Parties or at the request of the Commission a conference may be convened for the purpose of amending the present Convention.

Article 24   Amendments to the Annexes and the adoption of Annexes

1.   Any amendment to the Annexes proposed by a Contracting Party shall be communicated to the other Contracting Parties by the depositary government and considered in the Commission. If adopted by the Commission, the amendment shall be communicated to the Contracting Parties and recommended for acceptance.

2.   Such amendment shall be deemed to have been accepted at the end of a period determined by the Commission unless within that period any one of the

Contracting Parties has objected to the amendment. The accepted amendment shall enter into force on a date determined by the Commission.

The period determined by the Commission shall be prolonged for an additional period of six months and the date of entry into force of the amendment postponed accordingly, if, in exceptional cases, any Contracting Party before the expiring of the period determined by the Commission informs the depositary government, that, although it intends to accept the proposal, the constitutional requirements for such an acceptance are not yet fulfilled in its State.

3.   An Annex to the present Convention may be adopted in accordance with the provisions of this Article.

4.   The depositary government shall inform all Contracting Parties of any amendments or the adoption of a new Annex which enter into force under this Article and of the date on which such amendment or new Annex enters into force.

5.   Any objection under this Article shall be made by notification in writing to the depositary government which shall notify all Contracting Parties and the executive secretary of any such notification and the date of its receipt.

Article 25   *Reservations*

1.   The provisions of the present Convention shall not be subject to reservations.

2.   The provision of paragraph 1 of this Article does not prevent a Contracting Party from suspending for a period not exceeding one year the application of an Annex of the present Convention or part thereof or an amendment thereto after the Annex in question or the amendment thereto has entered into force.

3.   If after the entry into force of the present Convention a Contracting Party invokes the provisions of paragraph 2 of this Article it shall inform the other Contracting Parties, at the time of the adoption by the Commission of an amendment to an Annex, or a new Annex, of those provisions which will be suspended in accordance with paragraph 2 of this Article.

Article 26   *Signature, ratification, approval, and accession*

1.   The present Convention shall be open for signature in Helsinki on 22 March 1974 by the Baltic Sea States participating in the diplomatic conference

on the protection of the marine environment of the Baltic Sea area, held in Helsinki from 18 to 22 March 1974. The present Convention shall be open for accession to any other State interested in fulfilling the aims and purposes of the present Convention, provided that this State is invited by all the Contracting Parties.

The present Convention shall be open for accession by the European Economic Community. Within area of its competence, the European Economic Community is entitled to a number of votes equal to the number of its Member States which are Contracting Parties to the present Convention. The European Economic Community shall not exercise its rights to vote in cases where its Members exercise theirs and conversely.

2.   The present Convention shall be subject to ratification or approval by the States which have signed it.

3.   The instruments of ratification, approval, or accession shall be deposited with the Government of Finland, which will perform the duties of the depositary government.

Article 27   Entry into force

The present Convention shall enter into force two months after the deposit of the seventh instrument of ratification or approval.

For the European Economic Community acceding to the Convention according to Article 26 the Convention shall enter into force two months after the deposit of the instrument of accession.

Article 28   Withdrawal

1.   At any time after the expiry of five years from the date of entry into force of the present Convention any Contracting Party may, by giving written notification to the depositary government, withdraw from the present Convention. The withdrawal shall take effect for such Contracting Party on the 31st day of December of the year which follows the year in which the depositary government was notified of the withdrawal.

2.   In case of notification of withdrawal by a Contracting Party the depositary government shall convene a meeting of the Contracting Parties for the purpose of considering the effect of the withdrawal.

Article 29   *Language*

The present Convention has been drawn up in a single copy in the English language. Official translations into the Danish, Finnish, German, Polish, Russian and Swedish languages shall be prepared and deposited with the signed original.

In witness whereof the undersigned plenipotentiaries, being duly authorized thereto, have signed the present Convention.

Done at Helsinki, this twenty-second day of March one thousand nine hundred and seventy-four.

For Denmark:

HOLGER HANSEN

For Finland:

JERMU LAINE

For the German Democratic Republic:

HANS REICHELT

For the Federal Republic of Germany:

HANS-GEORG SACHS

For the Polish People's Republic:

JERZY KUSIAK

For Sweden:

SVANTE LUNDKVIST

For the Union of Soviet Socialist Republics:

E. E. ALEXEEVSKY

ANNEX I

HAZARDOUS SUBSTANCES

The protection of the Baltic Sea area from pollution by the substances listed below can involve the use of appropriate technical means, prohibitions and regulations of the transport, trade, handling, application, and final deposition of products containing such substances.

1)   DDT (1,1,1-trichloro-2,2-bis-(chlorophenyl)-ethane) and its derivatives DDE and DDD.

2)   PCB's (polychlorinated biphenyls).

3)   PCT's (polychlorinated terphenyls).

ANNEX II

NOXIOUS SUBSTANCES AND MATERIALS

The following substances and materials are listed for the purposes of Article 6 of the present Convention.

The list is valid for substances and materials introduced as waterborne into the marine environment. The Contracting Parties shall also endeavour to use best practicable means to prevent harmful substances and materials from being introduced as airborne to the Baltic Sea area.

A. **For urgent consideration:**

1) mercury, cadmium, and their compounds.

B.

2) Antimony, arsenic, beryllium, chronium, copper, lead, molybdenum, nickel, selenium, tin, vanadium, zinc, and their compounds, as well as elemental phosphorus.

3) Phenols and their derivatives.

4) Phthalic acid and its derivatives.

5) Cyanides.

6) Persistent halogenated hydrocarbons.

7) Polycyclic aromatic hydrocarbons and their derivatives.

8) Persistent toxic organosilicic compounds.

9) Persistent pesticides, including organophosphoric and organostannic pesticides, herbicides, slimicides and chemicals used for the preservation of wood, timber, wood pulp, cellulose, paper, hides and textiles, not covered by the provisions of Annex I to the present Convention.

10) Radioactive materials.

11) Acids, alkalis and surface active agents in high concentrations or big quantities.

12) Oil and wastes of petrochemical and other industries containing lipid-soluble substances.

13) Substances having adverse effects on the taste and/or smell of products for human consumption from the sea, or effects on taste, smell, colour, transparency or other characteristics of the water seriously reducing its amenity values.

14) Materials and substances which may float, remain in suspension or sink, and which may seriously interfere with any legitimate use of the sea.

15) Lignin substances contained in industrial waste waters.

16) The chelators EDTA (ethylenedinitrilotetraacetic acid or ethylenedi-aminetetraacetic acid) and DTPA diethylenetriaminopentaacetic acid).

ANNEX III

GOALS, CRITERIA AND MEASURES CONCERNING THE PREVENTION OF LAND-BASED POLLUTION

In accordance with the provisions of Article 6 of the present Convention the Contracting Parties shall endeavour to attain the goals and apply the criteria and measures enumerated in this Annex in order to control and minimize land-based pollution of the marine environment of the Baltic Sea area.

1) Municipal sewage shall be treated in an appropriate way so that the amount of organic matter does not cause harmful changes in the oxygen content of the Baltic Sea area and the amount of nutrients does not cause harmful eutrophication of the Baltic Sea area.

2) Municipal sewage shall also be treated in an appropriate way to ensure that the hygienic quality, and in particular epidemiological and toxicological safety, of the receiving sea area is maintained at a level which does not cause harm to human health, and in a way that under the given composition of the sewage no significant amount of such harmful substances as are listed in Annexes I and II to the present Convention is formed.

3) The polluting load of industrial wastes shall be minimized in an appropriate way in order to reduce the amount of harmful substances, organic matter and nutrients.

4) The means referred to in paragraph 3 of this Annex shall in particular include minimization of production of wastes by processing techniques, recirculation and reuse of processing water, developing of water economy and improvement of qualifications for water treatment. In the treatment of waste water mechanical, chemical, biological and other measures, according to the quality of the waste water, and as required to improve the quality of the recipient water, shall be applied.

5) The discharge of cooling water from nuclear power plants or other kinds of industries using large amounts of water shall be effected in a way which minimizes the pollution of the marine environment of the Baltic Sea area.

6) The Commission will define pollution control criteria, objectives for reduction of pollution and objectives concerning measures, including processing techniques and waste treatment, to reduce pollution of the Baltic Sea area.

ANNEX IV

PREVENTION OF POLLUTION FROM SHIPS

REGULATION 1

The Contracting Parties shall, in matters concerning the protection of the Baltic Sea area from pollution by ships, cooperate

(a) within the International Maritime Organization, in particular in promoting the development of international rules;

(b) in the effective and harmonized implementation of rules adopted by the International Maritime Organization.

REGULATION 2

The Contracting Parties shall, without prejudice to paragraph 4 of Article 4 of the present Convention, as appropriate assist each other in investigating violations of the existing legislation on anti-pollution measures, which have occurred or are suspected to have occurred within the Baltic Sea area. This assistance may include but is not limited to inspection by the competent authorities of oil record books, cargo record books, log books and engine log books and taking oil samples for analytical identification purposes.

REGULATION 3   Definitions

For the purposes of this Annex:

1)   'ship' means a vessel of any type whatsoever operating in the marine environment and includes hydrofoil boats, air-cushion vehicles, submersibles, floating craft and fixed or floating platforms;

2)   'administration' means the government of the State under whose authority the ship is operating. With respect to a ship entitled to fly a flag of any State, the administration is the government of that State. With respect to fixed or floating platforms engaged in exploration and exploitation of the sea bed and subsoil thereof adjacent to the coast over which the coastal State exercises sovereign rights for the purposes of exploration and exploitation of their natural resources, the administration is the government of the coastal State concerned;

3) a) 'discharge', in relation to harmful substances or effluents containing such substances, means any release howsoever caused from a ship and includes any escape, disposal, spilling, leaking, pumping, emitting or emptying;

b) 'discharge' does not include:

   i) dumping within the meaning of the Convention on the Prevention of Marine Pollution by Dumping of Wastes and Other Matter done at London on 29 December 1972; or

   ii) elease of harmful substances directly arising from the exploration, exploitation and associated off-shore processing of sea bed mineral resources; or

   iii) release of harmful substances for purposes of legitimate scientific research into pollution abatement or control;

4) 'nearest land': the term 'from the nearest land' means from the baseline from which the territorial sea of the territory in question is established in accordance with international law;

5) the term 'jurisdiction' shall be interpreted in accordance with international law in force at the time of application or interpretation of this Annex;

6) the term 'Marpol 73/78' means the international Convention for the prevention of pollution from ships, 1973, as modified by the Protocol of 1978 relating thereto.

REGULATION 4   Oil

The Contracting Parties, also being parties to Marpol 73/78, apply in conformity with that agreement the provisions of Annex I to Marpol 73/78 for the prevention of pollution by oil.

REGULATION 5   Noxious liquid substances

The Contracting Parties, also being parties to Marpol 73/78, apply in conformity with that agreement the provisions of Annex II to Marpol 73/78 for the prevention of pollution by noxious liquid substances carried in bulk.

REGULATION 6   *Harmful substances in packaged forms*

A.   The Contracting Parties shall as soon as possible apply suitable uniform rules for the carriage of harmful substances in packaged forms or in freight containers, portable tanks or road and rail tank wagons.

B.   With respect to certain harmful substances, as may be designated by the Commission, the master or owner of the ship or his representative shall notify the appropriate port authority of the intent to load or unload such substances at least 24 hours prior to such action.

C.   A report of an incident involving harmful substances shall be made in accordance with the provisions of Annex VI to the present Convention.

REGULATION 7   *Sewage*

The Contracting Parties shall apply the provisions of paragraphs A to D and F and G of this Regulation on discharge of sewage from ships while operating in the Baltic Sea area.

A.   Definitions

For the purposes of this Regulation:

1)   'sewage' means:

   a)   drainage and other wastes from any form of toilets, urinals, and WC scuppers;

   b)   drainage from medical premises (dispensary, sick bay, etc.) via wash basins, wash tubs and scuppers located in such premises;

   c)   drainage from spaces containing living animals; or

   d)   other waste waters when mixed with the drainages defined above;

2)   'holding tank' means a tank used for the collection and storage of sewage.

B.   Application

The provisions of this Regulation shall apply to:

   a)   ships of 200 tonnes gross tonnage and above;

   b)   ships of less than 200 tonnes gross tonnage which are certified to carry more than 10 persons;

   c) ships which do not have a measured gross tonnage and are certified to carry more than 10 persons.

C.   **Discharge of sewage**

1)   Subject to the provisions of paragraph D of this Regulation, the discharge of sewage into the sea is prohibited, except when:

   a) the ship is discharging comminuted and disinfected sewage using a system approved by the administration at a distance of more than four nautical miles from the nearest land, or sewage which is not comminuted or disinfected at a distance of more than 12 nautical miles from the nearest land, provided that in any case the sewage that has been stored in holding tanks shall not be discharged instantaneously but at a moderate rate when the ship is en route and proceeding at not less than four knots; or

   b) the ship has in operation a sewage treatment plant which has been approved by the administration, and

      i) the test results of the plant are laid down in a document carried by the ship;

      ii) additionally, the effluent shall not produce visible floating solids in, nor cause discolouration of the surrounding water; or

   c) the ship is situated in the waters under the jurisdiction of a State and is discharging sewage in accordance with such less stringent requirements as may be imposed by such State.

2)   When the sewage is mixed with wastes or waste water having different discharge requirements, the more stringent requirements shall apply.

D.   **Exceptions**

Paragraph C of this Regulation shall not apply to:

   a) the discharge of sewage from a ship necessary for the purpose of securing the safety of a ship and those on board or saving life at sea; or

   b) the discharge of sewage resulting from damage to a ship or its equipment if all reasonable precautions have been taken before and after the occurrence of the damage for the purpose of preventing or minimizing the discharge.

E.   **Reception facilities**

1)   Each Contracting Party undertakes to ensure the provision of facilities at its ports and terminals of the Baltic Sea area for the reception of

sewage, without causing undue delay to ships, adequate to meet the needs of the ship using them.

2) To enable pipes of reception facilities to be connected with the ship's discharge pipeline, both lines shall be fitted with a standard discharge connection in accordance with the following table:

Standard dimensions of flanges for discharge connections

Description	Dimension
Outside diamenter	210 mm
Inner diameter	According to pipe outside diameter
Bolt circle diameter	170 mm
Slots in flange	Four holes, 18 mm in diameter equidistantly placed on a bolt circle of the above diameter, slotted to the flange periphery. The slot width to be 18 mm.
Flange thickness	16 mm
Bolts and nuts: quantity and diameter	Four, each of 16 mm in diameter and of suitable length
The flange is designed to accept pipes up to a maximum internal diameter of 100 mm and shall be of steel or other equivalent material having a flat face. This flange, together with a suitable gasket, shall be suitable for a service pressure of 6 kg/cm'.	

For ships having a moulded depth of five metres and less, the inner diameter of the discharge connection may be 38 mm.

F. Surveys

1. Ships which are engaged in international voyages in the Baltic Sea area shall be subject to surveys specified below:

a) an initial survey before the ship is put in service or before the certificate required pursuant to paragraph G of this Regulation is issued for the first time, which shall include a survey of the ship which shall be such as to ensure:

i) when the ship is equipped with a sewage treatment plant the plant shall meet operational requirements based on standards and the test methods recommended by the Commission[1] and shall be approved by the administration;

ii) when the ship is fitted with a system to comminute and disinfect the sewage, such a system shall meet operational requirements based on standards and the test methods recommended by the commission[1] and shall be approved by the administration;

---

[1] (1) Reference is made to Helcom recommendation 1/5.

iii) when the ship is equipped with a holding tank the capacity of such tank shall be to the satisfaction of the administration for the retention of all sewage having regard to the operation of the ship, the number of persons on board and other relevant factors. The holding tank shall meet operational requirements based on standards and the test methods recommended by the Commission (1) and shall be approved by the administration; and

iv) that the ship is equipped with a pipeline to discharge sewage to a reception facility. The pipeline should be fitted with a standard shore connection in accordance with paragraph E or for ships in dedicated trades alternatively with other standards which can be accepted by the administration such as quick connection couplings.

This survey shall be such as to ensure that equipment, fittings, arrangements and material fully comply with the applicable requirements of this Regulation.

The administration shall recognize the 'certificate of type test' for sewage treatment plants issued under the authority of other Contracting Parties;

b) periodical surveys at intervals specified by the administration but not exceeding five years which shall be such as to ensure that the equipment, fittings, arrangements and material fully comply with the applicable requirements of this Regulation.

2) Surveys of the ship as regards enforcement of the provisions of this Regulation shall be carried out by officers of the administration. The administration may, however, entrust the surveys either to surveyors nominated for the purpose or to organizations recognized by it. In every case the administration concerned fully guarantees the completeness and efficiency of the surveys.

3) After any survey of the ship has been completed, no significant change shall be made in the equipment, fittings, arrangements, or material covered by the survey without the approval of the administration, except the direct replacement of such equipment or fittings.

G. Certificate

1) A sewage pollution prevention certificate shall be issued to ships certified to carry more than 50 persons which are engaged in international voyages in the Baltic Sea area, after survey in accordance with the provisions of paragraph F of this Regulation.

2)   Such certificate shall be issued either by the administration or by any person or organization duly authorized by it. In every case the administration assumes full responsibility for the certificate.

3)   The sewage prevention certificate shall be drawn up in the form corresponding to the model given in the appendix to Annex IV to Marpol 73/78, as the Contracting Parties are also parties to Marpol 73/78. If the language is not English, the text shall include a translation into English.

4)   A sewage pollution prevention certificate shall be issued for a period certified by the administration, which shall not exceed five years.

5)   A certificate shall cease to be valid if significant alternations have taken place in the equipment, fittings, arrangement or material required without the approval of the administration except the direct replacement of such equipment or fittings.

REGULATION 8   Garbage

The Contracting Parties, also being parties to Marpol 73/78, apply in conformity with that agreement the provisions of Annex V to Marpol 73/78 for the prevention of pollution by garbage from ships.

ANNEX V

EXCEPTIONS FROM THE GENERAL PROHIBITION OF DUMPING OF WASTE AND OTHER MATTER IN THE BALTIC SEA AREA

REGULATION 1

In accordance with paragraph 2 of Article 9 of the present Convention the prohibition of dumping shall not apply to the disposal at sea of dredged spoils provided that:

1) they do not contain significant quantities and concentrations of substances to be defined by the Commission and listed in Annexes I and II to the present Convention; and

2) the dumping is carried out under a prior special permit given by the appropriate national authority, either:

    a) within the area of the territorial sea of the Contracting Party; or

    b) outside the area of the territorial sea, whenever necessary, after prior consultations in the Commission.

When issuing such permits the Contracting Party shall comply with the provisions in Regulation 3 of this Annex.

REGULATION 2

1) The appropriate national authority referred to in paragraph 2 of Article 9 of the present Convention shall:

    a) issue special permits provided for in Regulation 1 of this Annex;

    b) keep records of the nature and quantities of matter permitted to be dumped and the location, time and method of dumping;

    c) collect available information concerning the nature and quantities of matter that has been dumped in the Baltic Sea area recently and up to the coming into force of the present Convention, provided that the dumped matter in question could be liable to contaminate water or organisms in the Baltic Sea area, to be caught by fishing equipment, or otherwise to give rise to harm, and the location, time and method of such dumping.

2)   The appropriate national authority shall issue special permits in accordance with Regulation 1 of this Annex in respect of matter intended for dumping in the Baltic Sea area:

    a)   loaded in its territory;

    b)   loaded by a vessel or aircraft registered in its territory or flying its flag, when the loading occurs in the territory of a State not party to the present Convention.

3)   When issuing permits under subparagraph 1 (a), the appropriate national authority shall comply with Regulation 3 of this Annex, together with such additional criteria, measures and requirements as they may consider relevant.

4)   Each Contracting Party shall report to the commission, and where appropriate to other Contracting Parties, the information specified in subparagraph 1 (c) of Regulation 2 of this Annex. The procedure to be followed and the nature of such reports shall be determined by the Commission.

REGULATION 3

When issuing special permits according to Regulation 1 of this Annex the appropriate national authority shall take into account:

1)   the quantity of dredged spoils to be dumped;

2)   the content of the matter referred to in Annexes I and II to the present Convention;

3)   location (e.g. coordinates of the dumping area, depth and distance from coast) and its relation to areas of special interest (e.g. amenity areas, spawning, nursery and fishing areas, etc.);

4)   water characteristics, if dumping is carried out outside the territorial sea, consisting of:

    a)   hydrographic properties (e.g. temperature, salinity, density, profile);

    b)   chemical properties (e.g. pH, dissolved oxygen, nutrients);

    c)   biological properties (e.g. primary production and benthic animals).

    The data should include sufficient information on the annual mean levels and the seasonal variation of the properties mentioned in this paragraph;

5)   the existence and effects of other dumping which may have been carried out in the dumping area.

REGULATION 4

Reports made in accordance with paragraph 5 of Article 9 of the present Convention shall include the following information:

1)   location of dumping, characteristics of dumped material, and counter-measures taken:

    a)   location (e.g. coordinates of the accidental dumping site, depth and distance from the coast);

    b)   method of deposit;

    c)   quantity and composition of dumped matter as well as its physical (e.g. solubility and density), chemical and biochemical (e.g. oxygen demand, nutrients), and biological properties (e.g. presence of viruses, bacteria, yeasts, parasites);

    d)   toxicity;

    e)   content of the substances referred to in Annex I and II to the present Convention;

    f)   dispersal characteristics (e.g. effects of currents and wind, and horizontal transport and vertical mixing);

    g)   water characteristics (e.g. temperature, pH, redox conditions, salinity and stratification);

    h)   bottom characteristics (e.g. topography, geological characteristics and redox conditions);

    i)   countermeasures taken and follow-up operations carried out or planned.

2)   general considerations and conditions:

    a)   possible effects on amenities (e.g. floating or stranded material, turbidity, objectionable odour, discolouration and foaming);

    b)   possible effects on marine life, fish and shellfish culture, fish stocks and fisheries, seaweed harvesting and cultures; and

    c)   possible effects on other uses of the sea (e.g. impairment of water quality for industrial use, underwater corrosion of structures, interference with ship operations from floating materials, interference with fishing or navigation and protection of areas of special importance for scientific or conservation purposes).

ANNEX VI

COOPERATION IN COMBATING MARINE POLLUTION

REGULATION 1

For the purpose of this Annex:

1) 'ship' means a vessel of any type whatsoever operating in the marine environment and includes hydrofoil boats, air-cushion vehicles, submersibles, floating craft and fixed or floating platforms;

2) 'administration' means the government of the State under whose authority the ship is operating. With respect to a ship entitled to fly a flag of any State, the administration is the government of that State. With respect to fixed or floating platforms engaged in exploration and exploitation of the sea bed and subsoil thereof adjacent to the coast over which the coastal State exercises sovereign rights for the purposes of exploration and exploitation of their natural resources, the administration is the government of the coastal State concerned;

3) a) 'discharge', in relation to harmful substances or effluents containing such substances, means any release howsoever caused from a ship and includes any escape, disposal, spilling, leaking, pumping, emitting or emptying;

   d) 'discharge' does not include:

   i) dumping within the meaning of the Convention on the Prevention of Marine Pollution by Dumping of Wastes and Other Matter done at London on 29 December 1972; or

   ii) release of harmful substances directly arising from the exploration, exploitation and associated off-shore processing of sea bed mineral resources; or

   iii) release of harmful substances for purposes of legitimate scientific research into pollution abatement or control.

REGULATION 2

The Contracting Parties undertake to maintain ability to combat spillages of oil and other harmful substances on the sea. This ability shall include adequate equipment, ships and manpower prepared for operations in coastal waters as well as on the high sea.

REGULATION 3

The Contracting Parties shall, without prejudice to paragraph 4 of Article 4 of the present Convention, develop and apply individually or in cooperation, surveillance activities covering the Baltic Sea area, in order to spot and monitor oil and other substances released into the sea.

REGULATION 4

In the case of loss overboard of harmful substances in packages, freight containers, portable tanks, or road and rail tank wagons, the Contracting Parties shall cooperate in the salvage and recovery of such packages, containers or tanks so as to minimize the danger to the environment.

REGULATION 5

1) The Contracting Parties, also being parties to the international Convention for the prevention of pollution from ships, 1973, as modified by the Protocol of 1978 relating thereto (Marpol 73/78), apply in conformity with that agreement the provisions of Article 8 and Protocol I to Marpol 73/78 on reports on incidents involving harmful substances. These provisions shall also be applied with regard to significant spillages of oil or other harmful substances in cases not covered by Article 8 of Marpol 73/78.

2) The Contracting Parties shall request masters of ships and pilots of aircraft to report without delay in accordance with this system on significant spillages of oil or other harmful substances observed at sea. Such reports should as far as possible contain the following data: time, position, wind and sea conditions, and kind, extent and probable source of the spill observed.

REGULATION 6

Each Contracting Party shall request masters of ships flying its flag to provide, in case of an incident, on request by the proper authorities, such detailed information about the ship and its cargo which is relevant to actions for preventing or combating pollution of the sea, and to cooperate with these authorities.

REGULATION 7

1) a)   The Contracting Parties shall as soon as possible agree bilaterally or multilaterally on those regions of the Baltic Sea area in which they will take action for combating or salvage activities whenever a significant spillage of oil or other harmful substances or any incidents causing or likely to cause pollution within the Baltic Sea area have occurred or are likely to occur. Such agreements shall not prejudice any other agreements concluded between Contracting Parties concerning the same subject. The neighbouring States shall ensure the harmonization of the different agreements. The Contracting Parties will inform each other about such agreements.

   The Contracting Parties may ask the Commission for assistance to reach agreement, if needed.

   b)   The Contracting Party within whose region a situation as described in Regulation 1 of this Annex occurs shall make the necessary assessments of the situation and take adequate action in order to avoid or minimize subsequent pollution effects and shall keep drifting parts of the spillage under observation until no further action is called for.

2)   In the case that such a spillage is drifting or is likely to drift into a region, where another Contracting Party should take action for purposes as defined in subparagraph 1 (a) of this Regulation, that Party shall without delay be informed of the situation and the actions that have been taken.

REGULATION 8

A Contracting Party requiring assistance for combating spillages of oil or other harmful substance at sea is entitled to call for assistance by other Contracting Parties, starting with those who seem likely also to be affected by the spillage. Contracting Parties called upon for assistance in accordance with this Regulation shall use their best endeavours to bring such assistance.

REGULATION 9

1)   The Contracting Parties shall provide information to the other Contracting Parties and the Commission about

   a)   their national organization for dealing with spillages at sea of oil and other harmful substances;

   b)   national regulations and other matters which have a direct bearing on combating pollution at sea by oil other harmful substances;

c) the competent authority responsible for receiving and dispatching reports of pollution at sea by oil and other harmful substances;

d) the competent authorities for dealing with questions concerning measures of mutual assistance, information and cooperation between the Contracting Parties according to this Annex;

e) actions taken in accordance with Regulation 8 of this Annex.

2.   The Contracting Parties shall exchange information of research and development programmes and results concerning ways in which pollution by oil and other harmful substances at sea may be dealt with and experiences in combating such pollution.

REGULATION 10

The authorities referred to in subparagraph 1 (d) of Regulation 9 of this Annex shall establish direct contact and cooperate in operational matters.

COUNCIL DECISION 94/157/EC[1]
of 21 February 1994
on the conclusion, on behalf of the Community, of the Convention on the Protection of the Marine Environment of the Baltic Sea Area (Helsinki Convention as revised in 1992)

THE COUNCIL OF THE EUROPEAN UNION,

Having regard to the Treaty establishing the European Community, and in particular Article 130s in conjunction with Article 228 (3), first subparagraph thereof,

Having regard to the proposal from the Commission[2],

Having regard to the opinion of the European Parliament[3],

Having regard to the opinion of the Economic and Social Committee[4],

Whereas the Commission, on behalf of the Community, took part in the negotiations of the drafting of the Helsinki Convention as revised in 1992;

Whereas that Convention was signed on behalf of the Community on 24 September 1992;

Whereas that Convention establishes a framework for regional cooperation to ensure the ecological rehabilitation of the Baltic Sea with a view to the self-regeneration of its marine environment and the preservation of its ecological balance;

Whereas the Community has adopted measures in the area covered by the Convention and should act at international level in that areas;

Whereas Community policy on the environment contributes to the pursuit of the objectives of preserving, protecting and improving the quality of the environment, protecting human health and the prudent and rational utilization of natural resources;

---

[1] OJ No L 73, 16, 3,1994, p. 19.
[2] OJ No C 226, 21. 8. 1993, p. 8.
[3] OJ No C 315, 22. 11. 1993.
[4] OJ No C 34, 2. 2. 1994, p. 5.

Whereas Community policy on the environment aims at a high level of protection; whereas it is based on the precautionary principle and on the principles that preventive action should be taken, that environmental damage should as a priority be recitfied at source and that the polluter should pay;

Whereas, within the framework of their respective responsibilities, the Community and the Member States cooperate with third countries and with competent international organizations;

Whereas the conclusion of the Convention by the Community will help attain the objectives set out in Article 130r of the Treaty,

HAS DECIDED AS FOLLOWS:

Article 1

The Convention on the Protection of the Marine Environment of the Baltic Sea Area (Helsinki Convention as revised in 1992), signed in Helsinki (Finland) on 24 September 1992, is hereby approved on behalf of the European Community.

The text of the Convention is attached to this Decision.

Article 2

The President of the Council shall deposit the instrument of approval with the Finnish Government in accordance with Article 38 of the Convention.

Done at Brussels, 21 February 1994.

For the Council

The President

Th. PANGALOS

CONVENTION
on the Protection of the Marine Environment of the Baltic Sea Area, 1992

THE CONTRACTING PARTIES,

CONSCIOUS of the indispensable values of the marine environment of the Baltic Sea area, its exceptional hydrographic and ecological characteristics and the sensitivity of its living resources to changes in the environment;

BEARING in mind the historical and present economic, social and cultural values of the Baltic Sea area for the well-being and development of the peoples of that region;

NOTING with deep concern the still ongoing pollution of the Baltic Sea area;

DECLARING their firm determination to assure the ecological restoration of the Baltic Sea, ensuring the possibility of self-regeneration of the marine environment and preservation of its ecological balance;

RECOGNIZING that the protection and enhancement of the marine environment of the Baltic Sea area are tasks that cannot effectively be accomplished by national efforts alone but by close regional cooperation and other appropriate international measures;

APPRECIATING the achievements in environmental protection within the framework of the 1974 Convention on the Protection of the Marine Environment of the Baltic Sea Area, and the role of the Baltic Marine Environment Protection Commission therein;

RECALLING the pertinent provisions and principles of the 1972 Declaration of the Stockholm Conference on the Human Environment and the 1975 Final Act of the Conference on Security and Cooperation in Europe (CSCE);

DESIRING to enhance cooperation with competent regional organizations such as the International Baltic Sea Fishery Commission established by the 1973 Gdansk Convention on Fishing and Conservation of the Living Resources in the Baltic Sea and the Belts;

WELCOMING the Baltic Sea Declaration by the Baltic and other interested States, the European Economic Community and cooperating international financial institutions assembled at Ronneby in 1990, and the Joint Comprehensive Programme aimed at a joint action plan in order to restore the Baltic Sea area to a sound ecological balance;

CONSCIOUS of the importance of transparency and public awareness as well as the work by non-governmental organizations for successful protection of the Baltic Sea area;

WELCOMING the improved opportunities for closer cooperation which have been opened by the recent political developments in Europe on the basis of peaceful cooperation and mutual understanding;

DETERMINED to embody developments in international environmental policy and environmental law into a new convention to extend, strengthen and modernize the legal regime for the protection of the marine environment of the Baltic Sea area;

HAVE AGREED as follows:

Article 1   *Convention area*

This Convention shall apply to the Baltic Sea area. For the purposes of this Convention the 'Baltic Sea area' shall be the Baltic Sea and the entrance to the Baltic Sea bounded by the parallel of the Skaw in the Skagerrak at 57°44'43'' N. It includes the internal waters, i.e, for the purpose of this Convention waters on the landward side of the base lines from which the breadth of the territorial sea is measured up to the landward limit according to the designation by the Contracting Parties.

A Contracting Party shall, at the time of the deposit of the instrument of ratification, approval or accession inform the depositary of the designation of its internal waters for the purposes of this Convention.

Article 2   *Definitions*

For the purposes of this Convention:

1)   'pollution' means introduction by man, directly or indirectly, of substances or energy into the sea, including estuaries, which are liable to create hazards to human health, to harm living resources and marine ecosystems, to cause hindrance to legitimate uses of the sea including fishing, to impair the quality for use of sea water, and to lead to a reduction of amenities;

2)   'pollution from land-based sources' means pollution of the sea by point or diffuse inputs from all sources on land reaching the sea waterborne, airborne or directly from the coast. It includes pollution from any delib-

erate disposal under the sea bed with access from land by tunnel, pipeline or other means;

3)   'ship' means a vessel of any type whatsoever operating in the marine environment and includes hydrofoil boats, air-cushion vehicles, submersibles, floating craft and fixed or floating platforms;

4) a) 'dumping' means:

    i) any deliberate disposal at sea or into the sea bed of wastes or other matter from ships, other man-made structures at sea or aircraft;

    ii) any deliberate disposal at sea of ships, other man-made structures at sea or aircraft;

  f) 'dumping' does not include:

    i) the disposal at sea of wastes or other matter incidental to, or derived from the normal operations of ships, other man-made structures at sea or aircraft and their equipment, other than wastes or other matter transported by or to ships, other man-made structures at sea or aircraft, operating for the purpose of disposal of such matter or derived from the treatment of such wastes or other matter on such ships, structures or aircraft;

    ii) placement of matter for a purpose other than the mere disposal thereof, provided that such placement is not contrary to the aims of the present Convention;

5)   'incineration' means the deliberate combustion of wastes or other matter at sea for the purpose of their thermal destruction. Activities incidental to the normal operation of ships or other man-made structures are excluded from the scope of this definition;

6)   'oil' means petroleum in any form including crude oil, fuel oil, sludge, oil refuse and refined products;

7)   'harmful substance' means any substance, which, if introduced into the sea, is liable to cause pollution;

8)   'hazardous substance' means any harmful substance which due to its intrinsic properties is persistent, toxic or liable to bio-accumulate,

9)   'pollution incident' means an occurrence or series of occurrences having the same origin, which results or may result in a discharge of oil or other harmful substances and which poses or may pose a threat to the marine environment of the Baltic Sea or to the coastline or related interests of one or more Contracting Parties, and which requires emergency actions or other immediate response;

10)   'regional economic integration organization' means any organization constituted by sovereign States, to which their member States have

transferred competence in respect of matters governed by this Convention, including the competence to enter into international agreements in respect of these matters;

11) the 'Commission' means the Baltic Marine Environment Protection Commission referred to in Article 19.

Article 3   *Fundamental principles and obligations*

1.   The Contracting Parties shall individually or jointly take all appropriate legislative, administrative or other relevant measures to prevent and eliminate pollution in order to promote the ecological restoration of the Baltic Sea area and the preservation of its ecological balance.

2.   The Contracting Parties shall apply the precautionary principle, i.e., to take preventive measures when there is reason to assume that substances or energy introduced, directly or indirectly, into the marine environment may create hazards to human health, harm living resources and marine ecosystems, damage amenities or interfere with other legitimate uses of the sea even when there is no conclusive evidence of a causal relationship between inputs and their alleged effects.

3.   In order to prevent and eliminate pollution of the Baltic Sea area the Contracting Parties shall promote the use of best environmental practice and best available technology. If the reduction of inputs, resulting from the use of best environmental practice and best available technology, as described in Annex II, does not lead to environmentally acceptable results, additional measures shall be applied.

4.   The Contracting Parties shall apply the polluter-pays principle.

5.   The Contracting Parties shall ensure that measurements and calculations of emissions from point sources to water and air and of inputs from diffuse sources to water and air are carried out in a scientifically appropriate manner in order to assess the state of the marine environment of the Baltic Sea area and ascertain the implementation of this Convention.

6.   The Contracting Parties shall use their best endeavours to ensure that the implementation of this Convention does not cause transboundary pollution in areas outside the Baltic Sea area. Furthermore, the relevant measures shall not lead either to unacceptable environmental strains on air quality and the atmosphere or on waters, soil and ground water, to unacceptably harmful or increasing waste disposal, or to increased risks to human health.

Article 4   Application

1.   This Convention shall apply to the protection of the marine environment of the Baltic Sea area which comprises the water-body and the sea bed including their living resources and other forms of marine life.

2.   Without prejudice to its sovereignty each Contracting Party shall implement the provisions of this Convention within its territorial sea and its internal waters through its national authorities.

3.   This Convention shall not apply to any warship, naval auxiliary, military aircraft or other ship and aircraft owned or operated by a State and used, for the time being, only on government non-commercial service.

However, each Contracting Party shall ensure, by the adoption of appropriate measures not impairing the operations or operational capabilities of such ships and aircraft owned or operated by it, that such ships and aircraft act in a manner consistent, so far as is reasonable and practicable, with this Convention.

Article 5   Harmful substances

The Contracting Parties undertake to prevent and eliminate pollution of the marine environment of the Baltic Sea area caused by harmful substances from all sources, according to the provisions of this Convention and, to this end, to implement the procedures and measures of Annex I.

Article 6   Principles and obligations concerning pollution from land-based sources

1.   The Contracting Parties undertake to prevent and eliminate pollution of the Baltic Sea area from land-based sources by using, inter alia, best environmental practice for all sources and best available technology for point sources. The relevant measures to this end shall be taken by each Contracting Party in the catchment area of the Baltic Sea without prejudice to its sovereignty.

2.   The Contracting Parties shall implement the procedures and measures set out in Annex III. To this end they shall, inter alia, as appropriate cooperate in the development and adoption of specific programmes, guidelines, standards or regulations concerning emissions and inputs to water and air, environmental quality, and products containing harmful substances and materials and the use thereof.

3.   Harmful substances from point sources shall not, except in negligible quantities, be introduced directly or indirectly into the marine environment of the Baltic Sea area, without a prior special permit, which may be periodically reviewed, issued by the appropriate national authority in accordance with the principles contained in Annex III, Regulation 3. The Contracting Parties shall ensure that authorized emissions to water and air are monitored and controlled.

4.   If the input from a watercourse, flowing through the territories of two or more Contracting Parties or forming a boundary between them, is liable to cause pollution of the marine environment of the Baltic Sea area, the Contracting Parties concerned shall jointly and, if possible, in cooperation with a third State interested or concerned, take appropriate measures in order to prevent and eliminate such pollution.

Article 7   Environmental impact assessment

1.   Whenever an environmental impact assessment of a proposed activity that is likely to cause a significant adverse impact on the marine environment of the Baltic Sea area is required by international law or supra-national regulations applicable to the Contracting Party of origin, that Contracting Party shall notify the Commission and any Contracting Party which may be affected by a transboundary impact on the Baltic Sea area.

2.   The Contracting Party of origin shall enter into consultations with any Contracting Party which is likely to be affected by such transboundary, impact, whenever consultations are required by international law or supranational regulations applicable to the Contracting Party of origin.

3.   Where two or more Contracting Parties share transboundary waters within the catchment area of the Baltic Sea, these Parties shall cooperate to ensure that potential impacts on the marine environment of the Baltic Sea area are fully investigated within the environmental impact assessment referred to in paragraph 1 of this Article. The Contracting Parties concerned shall jointly take appropriate measures in order to prevent and eliminate pollution including cumulative deleterious effects.

Article 8   Prevention of pollution from ships

1.   In order to protect the Baltic Sea area from pollution from ships, the Contracting Parties shall take measures as set out in Annex IV.

2.   The Contracting Parties shall develop and apply uniform requirements for the provision of reception facilities for ship-generated wastes, taking into

account, inter alia, the special needs of passenger ships operating in the Baltic Sea area.

Article 9   *Pleasure craft*

The Contracting Parties shall, in addition to implementing those provisions of this Convention which can appropriately be applied to pleasure craft, take special measures in order to abate harmful effects on the marine environment of the Baltic Sea area caused by pleasure craft activities. The measures shall, inter alia, deal with air pollution, noise and hydrodynamic effects as well as with adequate reception facilities for wastes from pleasure craft.

Article 10   *Prohibition of incineration*

1.   The Contracting Parties shall prohibit incineration in the Baltic Sea area.

2.   Each Contracting Party undertakes to ensure compliance with the provisions of this Article by ships:

a)   registered in its territory or flying its flag;

b)   loading, within its territory or territorial sea, matter which is to be incinerated; or

c)   believed to be engaged in incineration within its internal waters and territorial sea.

3.   In case of suspected incineration the Contracting Parties shall cooperate in investigating the matter in accordance with Regulation 2 of Annex IV.

Article 11   *Prevention of dumping*

1.   The Contracting Parties shall, subject to exemptions set forth in paragraphs 2 and 4 of this Article, prohibit dumping in the Baltic Sea area.

2.   Dumping of dredged material shall be subject to a prior special permit issued by the appropriate national authority in accordance with the provisions of Annex V.

3.   Each Contracting Party undertakes to ensure compliance with the provisions of this Article by ships and aircraft:

a)   registered in its territory or flying its flag;

b) loading, within its territory or territorial sea, matter which is to be dumped; or

c) believed to be engaged in dumping within its internal waters and territorial sea.

4. The provisions of this Article shall not apply when the safety of human life or of a ship or aircraft at sea is threatened by the complete destruction or total loss of the ship or aircraft, or in any case which constitutes a danger to human life, if dumping appears to be the only way of averting the threat and if there is every probability that the damage consequent upon such dumping will be less than would otherwise occur. Such dumping shall be so conducted as to minimize the likelihood of damage to human or marine life.

5. Dumping made under the provisions of paragrah 4 of this Article shall be reported and dealt with in accordance with Annex VII and shall be reported forthwith to the Commission in accordance with the provisions of Regulation 4 of Annex V.

6. In case of dumping suspected to be in contravention of the provisions of this Article the Contracting Parties shall cooperate in investigating the matter in accordance with Regulation 2 of Annex IV.

Article 12   Exploration and exploitation of the sea bed and its subsoil

1. Each Contracting Party shall take all measures in order to prevent pollution of the marine environment of the Baltic Sea area resulting from exploration or exploitation of its part of the sea bed and the subsoil thereof or from any associated activities thereon as well as to ensure that adequate preparedness is maintained for immediate response actions against pollution incidents caused by such activities.

2. In order to prevent and eliminate pollution from such activities the Contracting Parties undertake to implement the procedures and measures set out in Annex VI, as far as they are applicable.

Article 13   Notification and consultation on pollution incidents

1. Whenever a pollution incident in the territory of a Contracting Party is likely to cause pollution to the marine environment of the Baltic Sea area outside its territory and adjacent maritime area in which it exercises sovereign rights and jurisdiction according to international law, this Contracting Party

shall notify without delay such Contracting Parties whose interests are affected or likely to be affected.

2.   Whenever deemed necessary by the Contracting Parties referred to in paragraph 1, consultations should take place with a view to preventing, reducing and controlling such pollution.

3.   Paragraphs 1 and 2 shall also apply in cases where a Contracting Party has sustained such pollution from the territory of a third State.

Article 14   Cooperation in combating marine pollution

The Contracting Parties shall individually and jointly take, as set out in Annex VII, all appropriate measures to maintain adequate ability and to respond to pollution incidents in order to eliminate or minimize the consequences of these incidents to the marine environment of the Baltic Sea Area.

Article 15   Nature conservation and biodiversity

The Contracting Parties shall individually and jointly take all appropriate measures with respect to the Baltic Sea area and its coastal ecosystems influenced by the Baltic Sea to conserve natural habitats and biological diversity and to protect ecological processes. Such measures shall also be taken in order to ensure the sustainable use of natural resources within the Baltic Sea area. To this end, the Contracting Parties shall aim at adopting subsequent instruments containing appropriate guidelines and criteria.

Article 16   Reporting and exchange of information

1.   The Contracting Parties shall report to the Commission at regular intervals on:

a) the legal, regulatory, or other measures taken for the implementation of the provisions of this Convention, of its Annexes and of recommendations adopted thereunder;

b) the effectiveness of the measures taken to implement the provisions referred to in subparagraph (a) of this paragraph; and

c) problems encountered in the implementation of the provisions referred to in subparagraph (a) of this paragraph.

2.   On the request of a Contracting Party or of the Commission, the Contracting Parties shall provide information on discharge permits, emission data or data on environmental quality, as far as available.

Article 17   Information to the public

1.   The Contracting Parties shall ensure that information is made available to the public on the condition of the Baltic Sea and the waters in its catchment area, measures taken or planned to be taken to prevent and eliminate pollution and the effectiveness of those measures. For this purpose, the Contracting Parties shall ensure that the following information is made available to the public:

a)   permits issued and the conditions required to be met;

b)   results of water and effluent sampling carried out for the purposes of monitoring and assessment, as well as results of checking compliance with water-quality objectives or permit conditions; and

c)   water-quality objectives.

2.   Each Contracting Party shall ensure that this information shall be available to the public at all reasonable times and shall provide members of the public with reasonable facilities for obtaining, on payment of reasonable charges, copies of entries in its registers.

Article 18   Protection of information

1.   The provisions of this Convention shall not affect the right or obligation of any Contracting Party under its national law and applicable supra-national regulation to protect information related to intellectual property including industrial and commercial secrecy or national security and the confidentiality of personal data.

2.   If a Contracting Party nevertheless decides to supply such protected information to another Contracting Party, the Party receiving such protected information shall respect the confidentiality of the information received and the conditions under which it is supplied, and shall use that information only for the purposes for which it was supplied.

Article 19   Commission

1.   The Baltic Marine Environment Protection Commission, referred to as 'the Commission', is established for the purposes of this Convention.

2.   The Baltic Marine Environment Protection Commission, established pursuant to the Convention on the Protection of the Marine Environment of the Baltic Sea Area of 1974, shall be the Commission.

3.   The chairmanship of the Commission shall be given to each Contracting Party in turn in alphabetical order of the names of the Contracting Parties in the English language. The chairman shall serve for a period of two years, and cannot during the period of chairmanship serve as a representative of the Contracting Party holding the chairmanship.

Should the chairman fail to complete his term, the Contracting Party holding the chairmanship shall nominate a successor to remain in office until the term of that Contracting Party expires.

4.   Meetings of the Commission shall be held at least once a year upon convocation by the chairman. Extraordinary meetings shall, upon the request of any Contracting Party endorsed by another Contracting Party, be convened by the chairman to be held as soon as possible, however, not later than 90 days after the date of submission of the request.

5.   Unless otherwise provided under this Convention, the Commission shall take its decisions unanimously.

Article 20   The duties of the Commission

1.   The duties of the Commission shall be:

a) to keep the implementation of this Convention under continuous observation;

b) to make recommendations on measures relating to the purposes of this Convention;

c) to keep under review the contents of this Convention including its Annexes and to recommend to the Contracting Parties such amendments to this Convention including its Annexes as may be required including changes in the list of substances and materials as well as the adoption of new Annexes;

d) to define pollution control criteria, objectives for the reduction of pollution, and objectives concerning measures, particularly those described in Annex III;

e) to promote in close cooperation with appropriate governmental bodies, taking into consideration subparagraph (f) of this Article, additional measures to protect the marine environment of the Baltic Sea area and for this purpose:

    i) to receive, process, summarize and disseminate relevant scientific, technological and statistical information from available sources; and

    ii) to promote scientific and technological research; and

f) to seek, when appropriate, the services of competent regional and other international organizations to collaborate in scientific and technological research as well as other relevant activities pertinent to the objectives of this Convention.

2.   The Commission may assume such other functions as it deems appropriate to further the purposes of this Convention.

Article 21   Administrative provisions for the Commission

1.   The working language of the Commission shall be English.

2.   The Commission shall adopt its rules of procedure.

3.   The office of the Commission, known as 'the secretariat', shall be in Helsinki.

4.   The Commission shall appoint an executive secretary and make provisions for the appointment of such other personnel as may be necessary, and determine the duties, terms and conditions of service of the executive secretary.

5.   The executive secretary shall be the chief administrative official of the Commission and shall perform the functions that are necessary for the administration of this Convention, the work of the Commission and other tasks entrusted to the executive secretary by the Commission and its rules of procedure.

Article 22   Financial provisions for the Commission

1.   The Commission shall adopt its financial rules.

2.   The Commission shall adopt an annual or biennial budget of proposed expenditures and consider budget estimates for the fiscal period following thereafter.

3.   The total amount of the budget, including any supplementary budget adopted by the Commission shall be contributed by the Contracting Parties other than the European Economic Community, in equal parts, unless unanimously decided otherwise by the Commission.

4.   The European Economic Community shall contribute no more than 2,5 % of the administrative costs to the budget.

5.   Each Contracting Party shall pay the expenses related to the participation in the Commission of its representatives, experts and advisers.

Article 23   Right to vote

1.   Except as provided for in paragraph 2 of this Article, each Contracting Party shall have one vote in the Commission.

2.   The European Economic Community and any other regional economic integration organization, in matters within their competence, shall exercise their right to vote with a number of votes equal to the number of their member States which are Contracting Parties to this Convention. Such organizations shall not exercise their right to vote if their member States exercise theirs, and vice versa.

Article 24   Scientific and technological cooperation

1.   The Contracting Parties undertake directly, or when appropriate through competent regional or other international organizations, to cooperate in the fields of science, technology and other research, and to exchange data and other scientific information for the purposes of this Convention. In order to facilitate research and monitoring activities in the Baltic Sea area the Contracting Parties undertake to harmonize their policies with respect to permission procedures for conducting such activities.

2.   Without prejudice to Article 4 (2) of this Convention the Contracting Parties undertake directly, or when appropriate, through competent regional or other international organizations, to promote studies and to undertake, support or contribute to programmes aimed at developing methods assessing the nature and extent of pollution, pathways, exposures, risks and remedies in the Baltic Sea area. In particular, the Contracting Parties undertake to develop alternative methods of treatment, disposal and elimination of such matter and substances that are likely to cause pollution of the marine environment of the Baltic Sea area.

3.   Without prejudice to Article 4 (2) of this Convention the Contracting Parties undertake directly, or when appropriate through competent regional or other international organizations, and, on the basis of the information and data acquired pursuant to paragraphs 1 and 2 of this Article, to cooperate in developing inter-comparable observation methods, in performing baseline studies and in establishing complementary or joint programmes for monitoring.

4.   The organization and scope of work connected with the implementation of tasks referred to in the preceding paragraphs should primarily be outlined by the Commission.

Article 25   Responsibility for damage

The Contracting Parties undertake jointly to develop and accept rules concerning responsibility for damage resulting from acts or omissions in contravention of this Convention, including, inter alia, limits of responsibility, criteria and procedures for the determination of liability and available remedies.

Article 26   Settlement of disputes

1.   In case of a dispute between Contracting Parties as to the interpretation or application of this Convention, they should seek a solution by negotiation. If the Parties concerned cannot reach agreement they should seek the good offices of or jointly request mediation by a third Contracting Party, a qualified international organization or a qualified person.

2.   If the Parties concerned have not been able to resolve their dispute through negotiation or have been unable to agree on measures as described above, such disputes shall be, upon common agreement, submitted to an ad hoc arbitration tribunal, to a permanent arbitration tribunal, or to the International Court of Justice.

Article 27   Safeguard of certain freedoms

Nothing in this Convention shall be construed as infringing upon the freedom of navigation, fishing, marine scientific research and other legitimate uses of the high seas, as well as upon the right of innocent passage through the territorial sea.

Article 28   Status of Annexes

The Annexes attached to this Convention form an integral part of this Convention.

Article 29   Relation to other Conventions

The provisions of this Convention shall be without prejudice to the rights and obligations of the Contracting Parties under existing and future treaties which further and develop the general principles of the law of the sea underlying this Convention and, in particular, provisions concerning the prevention of pollution of the marine environment.

Article 30   Conference for the revision or amendment of the Convention

A conference for the purpose of a general revision of or an amendment to this Convention may be convened with the consent of the Contracting Parties or at the request of the Commission.

Article 31   Amendments to the Articles of the Convention

1.   Each Contracting Party may propose amendments to the Articles of this Convention. Any such proposed amendment shall be submitted to the depositary and communicated by it to all Contracting Parties, which shall inform the depositary of either their acceptance or rejection of the amendment as soon as possible after receipt of the communication.

A proposed amendment shall, at the request of a Contracting Party, be considered in the Commission. In such a case Article 19 (4) shall apply. If an amendment is adopted by the Commission, the procedure in paragraph 2 of this Article shall apply.

2.   The Commission may recommend amendments to the Articles of this Convention. Any such recommended amendment shall be submitted to the depositary and communicated by it to all Contracting Parties, which shall notify the depositary of either their acceptance or rejection of the amendment as soon as possible after receipt of the communication.

3.   The amendment shall enter into force 90 days after the Depositary has received notifications of acceptance of that amendment from all Contracting Parties.

Article 32   Amendments to the Annexes and the adoption of Annexes

1.   Any amendment to the Annexes proposed by a Contracting Party shall be communicated to the other Contracting Parties by the depositary and considered in the Commission. If adopted by the Commission, the amendment shall be communicated to the Contracting Parties and recommended for acceptance.

2.   Any amendment to the Annexes recommended by the Commission shall be communicated to the Contracting Parties by the depositary and recommended for acceptance.

3.   Such amendment shall be deemed to have been accepted at the end of a period determined by the Commission unless within that period any one of the Contracting Parties has, by written notification to the depositary, objected to the amendment. The accepted amendment shall enter into force on a date determined by the Commission.

The period determined by the Commission shall be prolonged for an additional period of six months and the date of entry into force of the amendment postponed accordingly, if, in exceptional cases, any Contracting Party informs the depositary before the expiration of the period determined by the Commission that, although it intends to accept the amendment, the constitutional requirements for such an acceptance are not yet fulfilled.

4.   An Annex to this Convention may be adopted in accordance with the provisions of this Article.

Article 33   Reservations

1.   The provisions of this Convention shall not be subject to reservations.

2.   The provision of paragraph 1 of this Article does not prevent a Contracting Party from suspending for a period not exceeding one year the application of an Annex to this Convention or part thereof or an amendment thereto after the Annex in question or the amendment thereto has entered into force. Any Contracting Party to the 1974 Convention on the Protection of the Marine Environment of the Baltic Sea Area, which upon the entry into force of this Convention, suspends the application of an Annex or part thereof, shall apply the corresponding Annex or part thereof to the 1974 Convention for the period of suspension.

3.   If after the entry into force of this Convention a Contracting Party invokes the provisions of paragraph 2 of this Article it shall inform the other Contracting Parties, at the time of the adoption by the Commission of an amendment to an Annex, or a new Annex, of those provisions which will be suspended in accordance with paragraph 2 of this Article.

Article 34   Signature

This Convention shall be open for signature in Helsinki from 9 April until 9 October 1992 by States and by the European Economic Community participating in the Diplomatic Conference on the Protection of the Marine Environment of the Baltic Sea Area held in Helsinki on 9 April 1992.

Article 35   Ratification, approval and accession

1.   This Convention shall be subject to ratification or approval.

2.   This Convention shall, after its entry into force, be open for accession by any other State or regional economic integration organization interested in fulfilling the aims and purposes of this Convention, provided that this State or organization is invited by all the Contracting Parties. In the case of limited competence of a regional economic integration organization, the terms and conditions of its participation may be agreed upon between the Commission and the interested organization.

3.   The instruments of ratification, approval or accession shall be deposited with the Depositary.

4.   The European Economic Community and any other regional economic integration organization which becomes a Contracting Party to this Convention shall in matters within their competence, on their own behalf, exercise the rights and fulfill the responsibilities which this Convention attributes to their member States. In such cases, the member States of these organizations shall not be entitled to exercise such rights individually.

Article 36   Entry into force

1.   This Convention shall enter into force two months after the deposit of the instruments of ratification or approval by all signatory States bordering the Baltic Sea and by the European Economic Community.

2.   For each State which ratifies or approves this Convention before or after the deposit of the last instrument of ratification or approval referred to in

paragraph 1 of this Article, this Convention shall enter into force two months after the date of deposit by such State of its instrument of ratification or approval or on the date of the entry into force of this Convention, whichever is the latest date.

3.	For each acceding State or regional economic integration organization this Convention shall enter into force two months after the date of deposit by such State or regional economic integration organization of its instrument of accession.

4.	Upon entry into force of this Convention the Convention on the Protection of the Marine Environment of the Baltic Sea Area, signed in Helsinki on 22 March 1974 as amended, shall cease to apply.

5.	Notwithstanding paragraph 4 of this Article, amendments to the Annexes of the said Convention adopted by the Contracting Parties to the said Convention between the signing of this Convention and its entry into force, shall continue to apply until the corresponding Annexes of this Convention have been amended accordingly.

6.	Notwithstanding paragraph 4 of this Article, recommendations and decisions adopted under the said Convention shall continue to be applicable to the extent that they are compatible with, or not explicitly terminated by this Convention or any decision adopted thereunder.

## Article 37	Withdrawal

1.	At any time after the expiry of five years from the date of entry into force of this Convention any Contracting Party may, by giving written notification to the depositary, withdraw from this Convention. The withdrawal shall take effect for such Contracting Party on the 30th day of June of the year which follows the year in which the depositary was notified of the withdrawal.

2.	In case of notification of withdrawal by a Contracting Party the depositary shall convene a meeting of the Contracting Parties for the purpose of considering the effect of the withdrawal.

## Article 38	Depositary

The Government of Finland, acting as depositary, shall:

a)	notify all Contracting Parties and the Executive Secretary of:

i)	the signatures;

ii) the deposit of any instrument of ratification, approval or accession;

iii) any date of entry into force of this Convention;

iv) any proposed or recommended amendment to any Article or Annex or the adoption of a new Annex as well as the date on which such amendment or new Annex enters into force;

v)   any notification, and the date of its receipt, pursuant to Articles 31 and 32;

vi) any notification of withdrawal and the date on which such withdrawal takes effect;

vii) any other act or notification relating to this Convention;

b) transmit certified copies of this Convention to acceding States and regional economic integration organizations.

In witness whereof the undersigned, being duly authorized thereto, have signed this Convention.

Done at Helsinki, this ninth day of April one thousand nine hundred and ninety-two in a single authentic copy in the English language which shall be deposited with the Government of Finland. The Government of Finland shall transmit certified copies to all Signatories.

ANNEX I

HARMFUL SUBSTANCES

PART 1: *GENERAL PRINCIPLES*

1.0. Introduction

In order to fulfil the requirements of relevant parts of this Convention the following procedure shall be used by the Contracting Parties in identifying and evaluating harmful substances, as defined in Article 2 (7).

1.1. Criteria on the allocation of substances

The identification and evaluation of substances shall be based on the intrinsic properties of substances, namely:

— persistency,

— oxicity or other noxious properties,

— endency to bio-accumulation,

as well as on characteristics liable to cause pollution, such as:

— the ratio between observed concentrations and concentrations having no observed effect,

— nthropogenically caused risk of eutrophication,

— ransboundary or long-range significance,

— isk of undesirable changes in the marine ecosystem and irreversibility or durability of effects,

— adioactivity,

— serious interference with harvesting of sea-foods or with other legitimate uses of the sea,

— istribution pattern (i.e. quantities involved, use pattern and liability to reach the marine environment),

— roven carcinogenic, teratogenic or mutagenic properties in or through the marine environment.

These characteristics are not necessarily of equal importance for the identification and evaluation of a particular substance or group of substances.

1.2.   Priority groups of harmful substances

The Contracting Parties shall, in their preventive measures, give priority to the following groups of substances which are generally recognized as harmful substances:

a) heavy metals and their compounds;

b) organohalogen compounds;

c) organic compounds of phosphorus and tin;

d) pesticides, such as fungicides, herbicides, insecticides, slimicides and chemicals used for the preservation of wood, timber, wood pulp, cellulose, paper, hides and textiles;

e) oils and hydrocarbons of petroleum origin;

f) other organic compounds especially harmful to the marine environment;

g) nitrogen and phosphorus compounds;

h) radioactive substances, including wastes;

i) persistent materials which may float, remain in suspension or sink;

j) substances which cause serious effects on taste and/or smell of products for human consumption from the sea, or effects on taste, smell, colour, transparency or other characteristics of the water.

PART 2:   BANNED SUBSTANCES

In order to protect the Baltic Sea area from hazardous substances, the Contracting Parties shall prohibit, totally or partially, the use of the following substances or groups of substances in the Baltic Sea area and its catchment area.

2.1.   Substances banned for all final uses, except for drugs

DDT (1,1,1-trichloro-2,2-bis-(chlorophenyl)-ethane) and its derivatives DDE and DDD.

2.2.   Substances banned for all uses, except in existing closed system equipment until the end of service life or for research, development and analytical purposes

a) PCB's (polychlorinated biphenyls);

b) PCT's (polychlorinated terphenyls).

2.3. Substances banned for certain applications

Organotin compounds for antifouling paints for pleasure craft under 25 m and fish net cages.

PART 3: PESTICIDES

In order to protect the Baltic Sea area from hazardous substances, the Contracting Parties shall endeavour to minimize and, whenever possible, to ban the use of the following substances as pesticides in the Baltic Sea area and its catchment area:

	CAS-number
Acrylonitrile	107131
Aldrin	309002
Aramite	140578
Cadmium compounds	—
Chlordane	57749
Chlordecone	143500
Chlordimeform	6164983
Chloroform	67663
1,2-Dibromoethane	106934
Dieldrin	60571
Endrin	72208
Fluoroacetic acid and derivatives	7664393, 144490
Heptachlor	76448
Isobenzane	297789
Isodrin	465736
Kelevan	4234791
Lead compounds	—

Mercury compounds	—
Morfamquat	4636833
Nitrophen	1836755
Pentachloropheno	187865
Polychlorinated terpenes	8001501
Quintozen	e82688
Selenium compounds	—
2,4,5-T	93765
Toxaphene	8001352

ANNEX II

CRITERIA FOR THE USE OF BEST ENVIRONMENTAL PRACTICE AND BEST AVAILABLE TECHNOLOGY

REGULATION 1: GENERAL PROVISIONS

1. In accordance with the relevant parts of this Convention the Contracting Parties shall apply the criteria for best environmental practice and best available technology described below.

2. In order to prevent and eliminate pollution the Contracting Parties shall use best environmental practice for all sources and best available technology for point sources, minimizing or eliminating inputs to water and air from all sources by providing control strategies.

REGULATION 2: BEST ENVIRONMENTAL PRACTICE

1. The term 'best environmental practice' is taken to mean the application of the most appropriate combination of measures. In selecting for individual cases, at least the following graduated range of measures should be considered:

— provision of information and education to the public and to users about the environmental consequences of choosing particular activities and products, their use and final disposal,

— he development and application of codes of good environmental practice covering all aspects of activity in the product's life,

— andatory labels informing the public and users of environmental risks related to a product, its use and final disposal,

— vailability of collection and disposal systems,

— aving of resources, including energy,

— ecycling, recovery and reuse,

— voiding the use of hazardous substances and products and the generation of hazardous waste,

— pplication of economic instruments to activities, products or groups of products and emissions,

— system of licensing involving a range of restrictions or a ban.

162

2.   In determining in general or individual cases what combination of measures constitute best environmental practice, particular consideration should be given to:

—   he precautionary principle,

—   he ecological risk associated with the product, its production, use and final disposal,

—   voidance or substitution by less polluting activities or substances,

—   cale of use,

—   otential environmental benefit or penalty of substitute materials or activities,

—   dvances and changes in scientific knowledge and understanding,

—   ime limits for implementation,

—   social and economic implications.

REGULATION 3:   BEST AVAILABLE TECHNOLOGY

1.   The term 'best available technology' is taken to mean the latest stage of development (state of the art) of processes, of facilities or of methods of operation which indicate the practical suitability of a particular measure for limiting discharges.

2.   In determining whether a set of processes, facilities and methods of operation constitute the best available technology in general or individual cases, special consideration should be given to:

—   comparable processes, facilities or methods of operation which have recently been successfully tried out,

—   technological advances and changes in scientific knowledge and under-standing,

—   the economic feasibility of such technology,

—   time limits for application,

—   the nature and volume of the emissions concerned,

—   non-waste/low-waste technology,

—   the precautionary principle.

REGULATION 4:   FUTURE DEVELOPMENTS

It therefore follows that 'best environmental practice' and 'best available technology' will change with time in the light of technological advances and economic and social factors, as well as changes in scientific knowledge and understanding.

ANNEX III

CRITERIA AND MEASURES CONCERNING THE PREVENTION OF POLLUTION FROM LAND-BASED SOURCES

REGULATION 1: GENERAL PROVISIONS

In accordance with the relevant parts of this Convention the Contracting Parties shall apply the criteria and measures in this Annex in the whole catchment area and take into account best environmental practice (BEP) and best available technology (BAT) as described in Annex II.

REGULATION 2: SPECIFIC REQUIREMENTS

1) Municipal sewage water shall be treated at least by biological or other methods equally effective with regard to reduction of significant parameters. Substantial reduction shall be introduced for nutrients.

2) Water management in industrial plants should aim at closed water systems or at a high rate of circulation in order to avoid waste water wherever possible.

3) Industrial waste waters should be separately treated before mixing with diluting waters.

4) Waste waters containing hazardous substances or other relevant substances shall not be jointly treated with other waste waters unless an equal reduction of the pollutant load is achieved compared to the separate purification of each waste water stream. The improvement of waste water quality shall not lead to a significant increase in the amount of harmful sludge.

5) Limit values for emissions containing harmful substances to water and air shall be stated in special permits.

6) Industrial plants and other point sources connected to municipal treatment plants shall use best available technology in order to avoid hazardous substances which cannot be made harmless in the municipal sewage treatment plant or which may disturb the processes in the plant. In addition, measures according to best environmental practice shall be taken.

7) Pollution from fish farming shall be prevented and eliminated by promoting and implementing best environmental practice and best available technology.

8) Pollution from diffuse sources, including agriculture, shall be eliminated by promoting and implementing best environmental practice.

9) Pesticides used shall comply with the criteria established by the Commission.

REGULATION 3: PRINCIPLES FOR ISSUING PERMITS FOR INDUSTRIAL PLANTS

The Contracting Parties undertake to apply the following principles and procedures when issuing the permits referred to in Article 6 (3) of this Convention:

1) The operator of the industrial plant shall submit data and information to
the appropriate national authority using a form of application. It is recommended that the operator negotiates with the appropriate national
authority concerning the data required for the application before sub-
mitting the application to the authority (agreement on the scope of
required information and surveys).

At least the following data and information shall be included in the
application:

General information

— name, branch, location and number of employees.

Actual situation and/or planned activities

— site of discharge and/or emission,
— type of production, amount of production and/or processing,
— production processes,
— type and amount of raw materials, agents and/or intermediate products,
— mount and quality of untreated waste water and raw gas from all
relevant sources (e.g. process water, cooling water),
— reatment of waste water and raw gas with respect to type, process and
efficiency of pre-treatment and/or final treatment,
— reated waste water and raw gas with respect to amount and quality at the
outlet of the pre-treatment and/or final treatment facilities,
— mount and quality of solid and liquid wastes generated during the
process and the treatment of waste water and raw gas,
— treatment of solid and liquid wastes,
— information about measures to prevent process failures and accidental
spills,
— present status and possible impact on the environment.

Alternatives and their various impacts concerning, e.g. ecological, economic and safety aspects, if necessary

— other possible production processes,

— other possible raw materials, agents and/or intermediate products,

— other possible treatment technologies.

2) The appropriate national authority shall evaluate the present status and potential impact of the planned activities on the environment.

3) The appropriate national authority issues the permit after comprehensive assessment with special consideration of the abovementioned aspects. At least the following shall be laid down in the permit:

— characterizations of all components (e.g. production capacity) which influence the amount and quality of discharge and/or emissions,

— limit values for amount and quality (load and/or concentration) of direct and indirect discharges and emissions,

— instructions concerning:

- construction and safety,

- production processes and/or agents,

- operation and maintenance of treatment facilities,

- recovery of materials and substances and waste disposal,

- type and extent of control to be performed by the operator (self-control),

- measures to be taken in case of process failures and accidental spills,

- analytical methods to be used,

- schedule for modernization, retrofitting and investigations done by the operator,

- schedule for reports of the operator on monitoring and/or self-control, retrofitting and investigation measures.

4) The appropriate national authority or an independent institution authorized by the appropriate national authority shall:

— inspect the amount and quality of discharges and/or emissions by sampling and analysing,

— control the attainment of the permit requirements,

— arrange monitoring of the various impacts of waste-water discharges and emissions into the atmosphere,

— review the permit when necessary.

ANNEX IV

PREVENTION OF POLLUTION FROM SHIPS

REGULATION 1:   COOPERATION

The Contracting Parties shall, in matters concerning the protection of the Baltic Sea area from pollution by ships, cooperate:

a) within the International Maritime Organization, in particular in promoting the development of international rules, based, inter alia, on the fundamental principles and obligations of this Convention which also includes the promotion of the use of best available technology and best environmental practice as defined in Annex II;

b) in the effective and harmonized implementation of rules adopted by the International Maritime Organization.

REGULATION 2:   ASSISTANCE IN INVESTIGATIONS

The Contracting Parties shall, without prejudice to Article 4 (3) of this Convention, assist each other as appropriate in investigating violations of the existing legislation on anti-pollution measures, which have occurred or are suspected to have occurred within the Baltic Sea area. This assistance may include but is not limited to inspection by the competent authorities of oil record books, cargo record books, log books and engine log books and taking oil samples for analytical identification purposes.

REGULATION 3:   DEFINITIONS

For the purposes of this Annex:

1) 'administration' means the government of the Contracting Party under whose authority the ship is operating. With respect to a ship entitled to fly a flag of any State, the administration is the government of that State. With respect to fixed or floating platforms engaged in exploration and exploitation of the sea bed and subsoil thereof adjacent to the coast over which the coastal State exercises sovereign rights for the purposes of exploration and exploitation of their natural resources, the administration is the government of the coastal State concerned;

2) a) 'discharge', in relation to harmful substances or effluents containing such substances, means any release howsoever caused from a ship and

includes any escape, disposal, spilling, leaking, pumping, emitting or emptying:

   c) 'discharge' does not include:

      i) dumping within the meaning of the Convention on the Prevention of Marine Pollution by Dumping of Wastes and Other Matter done at London on 29 December 1972; or

      ii) release of harmful substances directly arising from the exploration, exploitation and associated off-shore processing of sea-bed mineral resources; or

      iii) release of harmful substances for purposes of legitimate scientific research into pollution abatement or control;

3) the term 'from the nearest land' means from the baseline from which the territorial sea of the territory in question is established in accordance with international law;

4) the term 'jurisdiction' shall be interpreted in accordance with international law in force at the time of application or interpretation of this Annex;

5) the term 'Marpol 73/78' means the International Convention for the Prevention of Pollution from Ships, 1973, as modified by the Protocol of 1978 relating thereto.

REGULATION 4: APPLICATION OF THE ANNEXES TO MARPOL 73/78

Subject to Regulation 5 the Contracting Parties shall apply the provisions of the Annexes to Marpol 73/78.

REGULATION 5: SEWAGE

The Contracting Parties shall apply the provisions of paragraphs A to D and F and G of this Regulation on discharge of sewage from ships while operating in the Baltic Sea area.

A. Definitions

For the purposes of this Regulation:

1) 'sewage' means:

   a) drainage and other wastes from any form of toilets, urinals, and WC scuppers;

b) drainage from medical premises (dispensary, sick bay, etc.) via wash basins, wash tubs and scuppers located in such premises;

c) drainage from spaces containing living animals; or

d) other waste waters when mixed with the drainages defined above;

2) 'holding tank' means a tank used for the collection and storage of sewage.

B. Application

The provisions of this Regulation shall apply to:

a) ships of 200 tonnes gross tonnage and above;

b) ships of less than 200 tonnes gross tonnage which are certified to carry more than 10 persons;

c) ships which do not have a measured gross tonnage and are certified to carry more than 10 persons.

C. Discharge of sewage

1) Subject to the provisions of paragraph D of this Regulation, the discharge of sewage into the sea is prohibited, except when:

a) the ship is discharging comminuted and disinfected sewage using a system approved by the administration at a distance of more than four nautical miles from the nearest land, or sewage which is not comminuted or disinfected at a distance of more than 12 nautical miles from the nearest land, provided that in any case the sewage that has been stored in holding tanks shall not be discharged instantaneously but at a moderate rate when the ship is en route and proceeding at not less than four knots; or

b) the ship has in operation a sewage treatment plant which has been approved by the administration, and

i) the test results of the plant are laid down in a document carried by the ship;

ii) additionally, the effluent shall not produce visible floating solids in, nor cause discolouration of the surrounding water.

2) When the sewage is mixed with wastes or waste water having different discharge requirements, the more stringent requirements shall apply.

D.   Exceptions

Paragraph C of this Regulation shall not apply to:

a) the discharge of sewage from a ship necessary for the purpose of securing the safety of a ship and those on board or saving life at sea; or

b) the discharge of sewage resulting from damage to a ship or its equipment if all reasonable precautions have been taken before and after the occurrence of the damage for the purpose of preventing or minimizing the discharge.

E.   Reception facilities

1.   Each Contracting Party undertakes to ensure the provision of facilities at its ports and terminals of the Baltic Sea area for the reception of sewage, without causing undue delay to ships, adequate to meet the needs of the ships using them.

To enable pipes of reception facilities to be connected with the ship's discharge pipeline, both lines shall be fitted with a standard discharge connection in accordance with the following table:

Standard dimensions of flanges for discharge connections

Description	Dimension
Outside diameter	210 mm
Inner diameter	According to pipe outside diameter
Bolt circle diameter	170 mm
Slots in flange	Four holes 18 mm in diameter equidistantly placed on a bolt circle of the above diameter, slotted to the flange periphery. The slot width to be 18 mm
Flange thickness	16 mm
Bolts and nuts: quantity and diameter	Four, each of 16 mm in diameter and of suitable length
The flange is designed to accept pipes up to a maximum internal diameter of 100 mm and shall be of steel or other equivalent material having a flat face. This flange, together with a suitable gasket, shall be suitable for a service pressure of 6 kg/cm^2.	

For ships having a moulded depth of five meters and less, the inner diameter of the discharge connection may be 38 millimetres.

F.   Surveys

1)   Ships which are engaged in international voyages in the Baltic Sea area shall be subject to surveys as specified below:

a) an initial survey before the ship is put into service or before the certificate required pursuant to paragraph G of this Regulation is issued for the first time including a survey of the ship which shall be such as to ensure that:

i) when the ship is equipped with a sewage treatment plant the plant shall meet operational requirements based on the standards and test methods recommended by the Commission and shall be approved by the administration;

ii) when the ship is fitted with a system to comminute and disinfect the sewage, such system shall meet operational requirements based on the standards and test methods recommended by the Commission and shall be approved by the administration;

iii) when the ship is equipped with a holding tank the capacity of such tank shall be to the satisfaction of the administration for the retention of all sewage, having regard to the operation of the ship, the number of persons on board and other relevant factors. The holding tank shall meet operational requirements based on the standards and test methods recommended by the Commission and shall be approved by the administration; and

iv) the ship is equipped with a pipeline to discharge sewage to a reception facility. The pipeline should be fitted with a standard shore connection in accordance with paragraph E, or for ships in dedicated trades, alternatively with other standards which can be accepted by the administration such as quick connection couplings.

This survey shall be such as to ensure that equipment, fittings, arrangements and materials fully comply with the applicable requirements of this Regulation.

The administration shall recognize the 'certificate of type test' for sewage treatment plants issued under the authority of other Contracting Parties;

b) periodical surveys at intervals specified by the administration but not exceeding five years which shall be such as to ensure that the equipment, fittings, arrangements and materials fully comply with the applicable requirements of this Regulation.

2) Surveys of the ship as regards enforcement of the provisions of this Regulation shall be carried out by officers of the administration. The administration may, however, entrust the surveys either to surveyors nominated for the purpose or to organizations recognized by it. In every case the administration concerned fully guarantees the completeness and efficiency of the surveys.

3) After any survey of the ship has been completed, no significant change shall be made in the equipment, fittings, arrangements, or material covered by the survey without the approval of the administration, except the direct replacement of such equipment or fittings.

G. Certificate

1) A sewage pollution prevention certificate shall be issued to ships certified to carry more than 50 persons which are engaged in international voyages in the Baltic Sea area, after survey in accordance with the provisions of paragraph F of this Regulation.

2) Such certificate shall be issued either by the administration or by any person or organization duly authorized by it. In every case the administration assumes full responsibility for the certificate.

3) The sewage prevention certificate shall be drawn up in a form corresponding to the model given in the appendix to Annex IV to Marpol 73/78. If the language is not English, the text shall include a translation into English.

4) A sewage pollution prevention certificate shall be issued for a period certified by the administration, which shall not exceed five years.

5) A certificate shall cease to be valid if significant alterations have taken place in the equipment, fittings, arrangements or materials required without the approval of the administration except the direct replacement of such equipment or fittings.

ANNEX V

EXEMPTIONS FROM THE GENERAL PROHIBITION OF DUMPING OF WASTE AND OTHER MATTER IN THE BALTIC SEA AREA

REGULATION 1

In accordance with Article 11 (2) of this Convention the prohibition of dumping shall not apply to the disposal at sea of dredged materials provided that:

a) the dumping of dredged material containing harmful substances indicated in Annex I is only permitted according to the guidelines adopted by the Commission; and

b) the dumping is carried out under a prior special permit issued by the appropriate national authority, either:

   i) within the area of internal waters and the territorial sea of the Contracting Party; or

   ii) outside the area of internal waters and the territorial sea, whenever necessary, after prior consultations in the Commission.

When issuing such permits the Contracting Party shall comply with the provisions in Regulation 3 of this Annex.

REGULATION 2

1) The appropriate national authority referred to in Article 11 (2) of this Convention shall:

a) issue the special permits provided for in Regulation 1 of this Annex;

b) keep records of the nature and quantities of matter permitted to be dumped and the location, time and method of dumping;

c) collect available information concerning the nature and quantities of matter that has been dumped in the Baltic Sea area recently and up to the coming into force of this Convention, provided that the dumped matter in question could be liable to contaminate water or organisms in the Baltic Sea area, to be caught by fishing equipment, or otherwise to give rise to harm, and information concerning the location, time and method of such dumping.

2)   The appropriate national authority shall issue special permits in accordance with Regulation 1 of this Annex in respect of matter intended for dumping in the Baltic Sea area:

a)   loaded in its territory;

b)   loaded by a ship or aircraft registered in its territory or flying its flag, when the loading occurs in the territory of a State which is not a Contracting Party to this Convention.

3)   Each Contracting Party shall report to the Commission, and where appropriate to other Contracting Parties, the information specified in subparagraph 1 (c) of Regulation 2 of this Annex. The procedure to be followed and the nature of such reports shall be determined by the Commission.

REGULATION 3

When issuing special permits according to Regulation 1 of this Annex the appropriate national authority shall take into account:

a)   the quantity of dredged material to be dumped;

b)   the content of harmful substances as referred to in Annex I;

c)   the location (e.g. coordinates of the dumping area, depth and distance from the coast) and its relation to areas of special interest (e.g. amenity areas, spawning, nursery and fishing areas, etc.);

d)   the water characteristics, if dumping is carried out outside the territorial sea, consisting of:

i) hydrographic properties (e.g. temperature, salinity, density, profile);

ii) chemical properties (e.g. pH, dissolved oxygen, nutrients);

iii) biological properties (e.g. primiary production and benthic animals);

the data should include sufficient information on the annual mean levels and seasonal variation of the properties mentioned in this paragraph; and

e)   the existence and effects of other dumping which may have been carried out in the dumping area.

REGULATION 4

Reports made in accordance with Article 11 (5) of this Convention shall include the information to be provided in the reporting form to be determined by the Commission.

ANNEX VI

PREVENTION OF POLLUTION FROM OFFSHORE ACTIVITIES

REGULATION 1: DEFINITIONS

For the purposes of this Annex:

1) 'offshore activity' means any exploration and exploitation of oil and gas by a fixed or floating offshore installation or structure including all associated activities thereon;

2) 'offshore unit' means any fixed or floating offshore installation or structure engaged in gas or oil exploration, exploitation or production activities, or loading or unloading of oil;

3) 'exploration' includes any drilling activity but not seismic investigations;

4) 'exploitation' includes any production, well testing or stimulation activity.

REGULATION 2: USE OF BEST AVAILABLE TECHNOLOGY AND BEST ENVIRONMENTAL PRACTICE

The Contracting Parties undertake to prevent and eliminate pollution from offshore activities by using the principles of best available technology and best environmental practice as defined in Annex II.

REGULATION 3: ENVIRONMENTAL IMPACT ASSESSMENT AND MONITORING

1) An environmental impact assessment shall be made before an offshore activity is permitted to start. In case of exploitation referred to in Regulation 5 the outcome of this assessment shall be notified to the Commission before the offshore activity is permitted to start.

2) In connection with the environmental impact assessment the environmental sensitivity of the sea area around a proposed offshore unit should be assessed with respect to the following:

   a) the importance of the area for birds and marine mammals;

   b) (b) the importance of the area as fishing or spawning grounds for fish and shellfish, and for aquaculture;

    c) the recreational importance of the area;

    d) the composition of the sediment measured as: grain size distribution, dry matter, ignition loss, total hydrocarbon content, and Ba, Cr, Pb, Cu, Hg and Cd content;

    e) the abundance and diversity of benthic fauna and the content of selected aliphatic and aromatic hydrocarbons.

3)   In order to monitor the consequent effects of the exploration phase of the offshore activity studies, at least those referred to in subparagraph (d), shall be carried out before and after the operation.

4)   In order to monitor the consequent effects of the exploitation phase of the offshore activity studies, at least those referred to in subparagraphs (d) and (e), shall be carried out before the operation, at annual intervals during the operation, and after the operation has been concluded.

REGULATION 4:   *DISCHARGES ON THE EXPLORATION PHASE*

1.   The use of oil-based drilling mud or muds containing other harmful substances shall be restricted to cases where it is necessary for geological, technical or safety reasons and only after prior authorization by the appropriate national authority. In such cases appropriate measures shall be taken and appropriate installations provided in order to prevent the discharge of such muds into the marine environment.

2.   2. Oil-based drilling muds and cuttings arising from the use of oil-based drilling muds should not be discharged in the Baltic Sea area but taken ashore for final treatment or disposal in an environmentally acceptable manner.

3.   3. The discharge of water-based mud and cuttings shall be subject to authorization by the appropriate national authority. Before authorization the content of the water-based mud must be proven to be of low toxicity.

4.   4. The discharge of cuttings arising from the use of water-based drilling mud shall not be permitted in specifically sensitive parts of the Baltic Sea area such as confined or shallow areas with limited water exchange and areas characterized by rare, valuable or particularly fragile ecosystems.

REGULATION 5: DISCHARGES ON THE EXPLOITATION PHASE

In addition to the provisions of Annex IV the following provisions shall apply to discharges:

a) all chemicals and materials shall be taken ashore and may be discharged only exceptionally after obtaining permission from the appropriate national authority in each individual operation;

b) the discharge of production water and displacement water is prohibited unless its oil content is proven to be less than 15 mg/l measured by the methods of analysis and sampling to be adopted by the Commission;

c) if compliance with this limit value cannot be achieved by the use of best environmental practice and best available technology the appropriate national authority may require adequate additional measures to prevent possible pollution of the marine environment of the Baltic Sea area and allow, if necessary, a higher limit value which shall, however, be as low as possible and in no case exceed 40 mg/l; the oil content shall be measured as provided in subparagraph (b);

d) the permitted discharge shall not, in any case, create any unacceptable effects on the marine environment;

e) in order to benefit from the future development in cleaning and production technology, discharge permits shall be regularly reviewed by the appropriate national authority and the discharge limits shall be revised accordingly.

REGULATION 6: REPORTING PROCEDURE

Each Contracting Party shall require that the operator or any other person having charge of the offshore unit shall report in accordance with the provisions of Regulation 5 (1) of Annex VII to this Convention.

REGULATION 7: CONTINGENCY PLANNING

Each offshore unit shall have a pollution emergency plan approved in accordance with the procedure established by the appropriate national authority. The plan shall contain information on alarm and communication systems, organization of response measures, a list of prepositioned equipment and a description of the measures to be taken in different types of pollution incidents.

REGULATION 8: DISUSED OFFSHORE UNITS

The Contracting Parties shall ensure that abandoned, disused offshore units and accidentally wrecked offshore units are entirely removed and brought ashore under the responsibility of the owner and that disused drilling wells are plugged.

REGULATION 9: EXCHANGE OF INFORMATION

The Contracting Parties shall continuously exchange information through the Commission on the location and nature of all planned or accomplished offshore activities and on the nature and amounts of discharges as well as on contingency measures that are undertaken.

ANNEX VII

RESPONSE TO POLLUTION INCIDENTS

REGULATION 1: GENERAL PROVISIONS

1) The Contracting Parties undertake to maintain the ability to respond to pollution incidents threatening the marine environment of the Baltic Sea area. This ability shall include adequate equipment, ships and manpower prepared for operations in coastal waters as well as on the high sea.

2) a) In addition to the incidents referred to in Article 13 the Contracting Party shall also notify without delay those pollution incidents occuring within its response region, which affect or are likely to affect the interests of other Contracting Parties.

   b) In the event of a significant pollution incident other Contracting Parties and the Commission shall also be informed as soon as possible.

3) The Contracting Parties agree that subject to their capabilities and the availability of relevant resources, they shall cooperate in responding to pollution incidents when the severity of such incidents so justify.

4. In addition the Contracting Parties shall take other measures to:

   a) conduct regular surveillance outside their coastlines; and

   b) otherwise cooperate and exchange information with other Contracting Parties in order to improve the ability to respond to pollution incidents.

REGULATION 2: CONTINGENCY PLANNING

Each Contracting Party shall draw up a national contingency plan and in cooperation with other Contracting Parties, as appropriate, bilateral or multilateral plans for a joint response to pollution incidents.

REGULATION 3: SURVEILLANCE

1. In order to prevent violations of the existing regulations on prevention of pollution from ships the Contracting Parties shall develop and apply individually or in cooperation, surveillance activities covering the Baltic Sea area in order to spot and monitor oil and other substances released into the sea.

2.   The Contracting Parties shall undertake appropriate measures to conduct the surveillance referred to in paragraph 1 by using, inter alia, airborne surveillance equipped with remote sensing systems.

REGULATION 4:   RESPONSE REGIONS

The Contracting Parties shall as soon as possible agree bilaterally or multilaterally on those regions of the Baltic Sea area in which they shall conduct surveillance activities and take action to respond whenever a significant pollution incident has occurred or is likely to occur. Such agreements shall not prejudice any other agreements concluded between Contracting Parties concerning the same subject. Neighbouring States shall ensure the harmonization of different agreements. Contracting Parties shall inform other Contracting Parties and the Commission about such agreements.

REGULATION 5:   REPORTING PROCEDURE

1) a) Each Contracting Party shall require masters or other persons having charge of ships flying its flag to report without delay any event on their ship involving a discharge or probable discharge of oil or other harmful substances.

   b) The report shall be made to the nearest coastal State and in accordance with the provisions of Article 8 and Protocol I of the International Convention for the Prevention of Pollution from Ships, 1973, as modified by the Protocol of 1978 related thereto (Marpol 73/78).

   a) The Contracting Parties shall request masters or other persons having charge of ships and pilots of aircraft to report without delay and in accordance with this system on significant spillages of oil or other harmful substances observed at sea. Such reports should as far as possible contain the following data: time, position, wind and sea conditions, and kind, extent and probable source of the spill observed.

2)   The provisions of paragraph 1 (b) shall also be applied with regard to dumping made under the provisions of Article 11 (4) of this Convention.

REGULATION 6: EMERGENCY MEASURES ON BOARD SHIPS

1.   Each Contracting Party shall require that ships entitled to fly its flag have on board a shipboard oil pollution emergency plan as required by and in accordance with the provisions of Marpol 73/78.

2.   Each Contracting Party shall request masters of ships flying its flag or, in case of fixed or floating platforms operating under its jurisdiction, the persons having charge of platforms to provide, in case of a pollution incident and on request by the proper authorities, such detailed information about the ship and its cargo or in case of platform its production which is relevant to actions for preventing or responding to pollution of the sea, and to cooperate with these authorities.

REGULATION 7: RESPONSE MEASURES

1)   The Contracting Party shall, when a pollution incident occurs in its response region, make the necessary assessments of the situation and take adequate response action in order to avoid or minimize subsequent pollution effects.

2) a)   The Contracting Parties shall, subject to subparagraph (b), use mechanical means to respond to pollution incidents.

   b)   Chemical agents may be used only in exceptional cases and after authorization, in each individual case, by the appropriate national authority.

3)   When such a spillage is drifting or is likely to drift into a response region of another Contracting Party, that Party shall without delay be informed of the situation and the actions that have been taken.

REGULATION 8: ASSISTANCE

1)   According to the provisions of paragraph 3 of Regulation 1:

   a)   a Contracting Party is entitled to call for assistance by other Contracting Parties when responding to a pollution incident at sea; and

   b)   Contracting Parties shall use their best endeavours to bring such assistance.

2)   Contracting Parties shall take necessary legal or administrative measures to facilitate:

a) the arrival and utilization in and departure from its territory of ships, aircraft and other modes of transport engaged in responding to a pollution incident or transporting personnel, cargoes, materials and equipment required to deal with such an incident; and

b) the expeditious movement into, through, and out of its territory of personnel, cargoes, materials and equipment referred to in subparagraph (a).

REGULATION 9: REIMBURSEMENT OF COST OF ASSISTANCE

1) The Contracting Parties shall bear the costs of assistance referred to in Regulation 8 in accordance with this Regulation.

2) a) If the action was taken by one Contracting Party at the express request of another Contracting Party, the requesting Party shall reimburse to the assisting Party the costs of the action of the assisting Party. If the request is cancelled the requesting Party shall bear the costs already incurred or committed by the assisting Party.

c) If the action was taken by a Contracting Party on its own initiative, this Party shall bear the costs of its action.

d) The principles laid down above in subparagraphs (a) and (b) shall apply unless the Parties concerned otherwise agree in any individual case.

3) Unless otherwise agreed, the costs of the action taken by a Contracting Party at the request of another Party shall be fairly calculated according to the law and current practice of the assisting Party concerning the reimbursement of such costs.

4) The provisions of this Regulation shall not be interpreted as in any way prejudicing the rights of Contracting Parties to recover from third parties the costs of actions taken to deal with pollution incidents under other applicable provisions and rules of international law and national or supra-national regulations.

REGULATION 10: REGULAR COOPERATION

1) Each Contracting Party shall provide information to the other Contracting Parties and the Commission about:

a) its organization for dealing with spillages at sea of oil and other harmful substances;

b) its regulations and other matters which have a direct bearing on preparedness and response to pollution at sea by oil and other harmful substances;

c) the competent authority responsible for receiving and dispatching reports of pollution at sea by oil and other harmful substances;

d) the competent authorities for dealing with questions concerning measures for mutual assistance, information and cooperation between the Contracting Parties according to this Annex; and

e) actions taken in accordance with Regulations 7 and 8 of this Annex.

2) The Contracting Parties shall exchange information on research and development programmes, results concerning ways in which pollution by oil and other harmful substances at sea may be dealt with and experiences in surveillance activities and in responding to such pollution.

3) The Contracting Parties shall on a regular basis arrange joint operational combating exercises as well as alarm exercises.

4) The Contracting Parties shall cooperate within the International Maritime Organization in matters concerning the implementation and further development of the International Convention on Oil Pollution Preparedness, Response and Cooperation.

REGULATION 11:   HELCOM COMBATING MANUAL

The Contracting Parties agree to apply, as far as practicable, the principles and rules included in the Manual on Cooperation in Combating Marine Pollution, detailing this Annex and adopted by the Commission or by the Committee designated by the Commission for this purpose.

COUNCIL RESOLUTION 94/C 135/02[1]
of 6 May 1994
on a Community strategy, for integrated coastal-zone management

THE COUNCIL OF THE EUROPEAN UNION,

RECALLS its resolution of 25 February 1992 on the future Community policy concerning the European coastal zone[2];

UNDERLINES once more the need for a Community strategy for the integrated management and development of coastal zones, based on the principles of sustainability and sound ecological and environmental practice;

RECALLS that such a strategy is also provided for under the fifth Community programme of policy and action in relation to the environment and sustainable developmen[3], which singles out coastal zone management and conservation as a priority matter, and EMPHASIZES in this connection that this task should be undertaken in a spirit of responsibility-sharing;

WELCOMES the progress already made by several Member States at national level towards the implementation of an integrated coastal zone management strategy;

RECOGNIZES also the contribution that a number of existing Community measures, including the implementation of Council Directive 79/409/EEC of 2 April 1979 on the conservation of wild birds[4], Council Directive 85/337/EEC of 27 June 1985 on the assessment of the effects of certain public and private projects on the environment[5] and Council Directive 92/43/EEC of 21 May 1992 on the conservation of natural habitats and of wild flora and fauna[6] together with the use of certain appropriate financial instruments, could make to such a strategy;

RENEWS its invitation to the Commission to propose within six months at the latest, with a view to strengthening coordinated action in this area and in accordance with the principle of subsidiarity, a Community strategy for the

---

[1] OJ No C 135, 18. 5. 1994, p. 2.
[2] OJ No C 59, 6. 3. 1992, p. 1.
[3] OJ No C 138, 17. 5. 1993, p. 1.
[4] OJ No L 103, 25. 4. 1979, p. 1.
[5] OJ No L 175, 5. 7. 1985, p. 40.
[6] OJ No L 206, 22. 7. 1992, p. 7.

integrated management of the whole of the Community coastline that, while taking account of the specific problems and potential of the diffrent zones, will provide a framework for its conservation and sustainable use;

UNDERTAKES to examine such a proposal as soon as it is submitted as a matter of priority and with a view to introducing possible additional Community action;

INVITES the Member States to strengthen their own efforts with a view to further increasing the protection of coastal zones throughout the Community.

European Commission

**European Community environment legislation
Volume 7 — Water**

Luxembourg: Office for Official Publications of the European Communities

1996 — I, 187 pp. — 16.2 x 22.9 cm

ISBN 92-827-6891-0 (Volume 7)
ISBN 92-827-6828-7 (Volumes 1-7)

Price (excluding VAT) in Luxembourg: ECU 11 (Volume 7)
ECU 74 (Volumes 1-7)